1m4(10

- 9 NOV 2011

07 AUG 2012

2 2 MAY 2013

2 3 DEC 2014

31 May 22

21 Jun 22

2 1 JUN 2022

12 Jul 22 ain

10 - 8 · 2022 P

First published 2009
© Trevor Yorke 2009

COUNTRYSIDE BOOKS
3 Catherine Road
Newbury, Berkshire

To view our complete range of books,
please visit us at
www.countrysidebooks.co.uk

ISBN 978 1 84674 146 3

*To Dad
without whose enthusiasm
and knowledge this book
would never have been written*

Photographs by the author and Stan Yorke
Illustrations by Trevor Yorke, with thanks to
Megan Hulme for the use of her hands in Fig 8.13

Designed by Peter Davies, Nautilus Design
Produced through MRM Associates Ltd., Reading
Typeset by CJWT Solutions, St Helens
Printed in Thailand

CONTENTS

Introduction

✦

Winding tranquil waters mirroring trees and foliage occasionally crossed by rustic arched bridges. Flights of locks stepping up through a patchwork of fields or down into a major city dwarfed by imposing mills and offices. Spectacular aqueducts upon which a narrow channel of water seemingly flies across the awestruck valley below. The images conjured up by the thought of English canals are evocative; these unique spaces so close to the modern world yet such an escape from it attract millions each year, from first time boaters to Hollywood film stars! But these idyllic settings have a rather hollow effect without the key by which they are unlocked, narrowboats. It is the colourful craft glistening with polished brass and contrasting bold paint schemes that are the stars of the show. It is the distinctive chugging noise, graceful gliding through the water and smoke rising from chimneys that makes the traditional narrowboat an icon and its modern cruiser counterpart ideal for weekend breaks, holidays or even as a home.

Although we are all familiar with these images, what are the boats we see really like? When did the traditional narrowboat first appear and how did a family cope with living and working aboard? How were the boats built and what are the differences between the various types? Are modern narrowboats different and what is the best way to approach hiring, buying or living on them? Most of us have at some time looked enviously at boaters passing through locks, but how do these work and what are the secrets of cruising on narrowboats?

It is these questions and more that this book seeks to answer by using photographs, diagrams and drawings. The surprising history of narrowboats is described in the first section in three easy to follow stages, explaining where the craft you see came from, what they originally looked like and how they were used. The second section goes into detail about the different parts of traditional and modern narrowboats from the hull and superstructure down to the colourful decoration that makes them so unique. The final two chapters give tips on hiring, buying and living on a boat and a first timer's guide to cruising on the canals.

Whether you are a newcomer, an experienced boater or someone who would just like to know a little more about the canals they stand watching (onlookers known to boaters as 'gongoozlers') this book will hopefully surprise and inform. It is packed with facts, advice and warnings gained from the first-hand experience of our family who have been boating since the 1960s. If at times these details seem overwhelming then please do not be put off, even in our most calamitous moments on the water the canals and the boats we cruised on never ceased to charm us with their beauty and pacify us with their tranquillity. One important word, though, before turning over the next page – never call today's boats 'barges' – that's like calling a Ferrari 'a lorry'! Just refer to them as narrowboats and you are halfway to being a boater!

Trevor Yorke

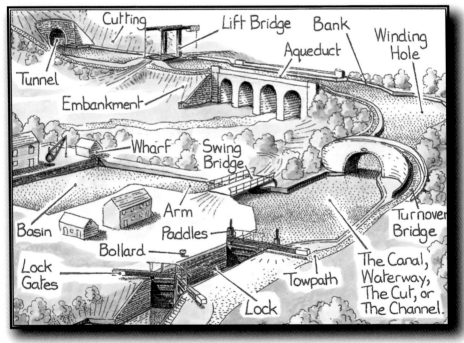

Some of the features you will see along a canal.

SECTION I

THE HISTORY OF NARROWBOATS

CHAPTER I

The Rise of the Canals
1760–1830

FIG 1.1: BLACK COUNTRY MUSEUM, DUDLEY, WEST MIDLANDS: *A busy industrial scene recreated at this excellent living museum, which gives an accurate impression of the surroundings through which working narrowboats plied their trade in the heyday of canals. It was muck, grime, smoke and noise, far from the tranquil retreat that attracts people today.*

Today as we watch or cruise on a colourfully decorated narrowboat, gliding silently through tranquil waters and lush green surroundings, we are enjoying a scene generally created in the 20th century. Nature's amazing ability to claim back that which was so savagely beaten and choked by industry has covered the true origins and appearance of our waterways. The canals have become a place of escape and beauty, but in the past this was far from the case.

When first conceived and built they were at the forefront of technology; their reliable service and relative speed transformed towns through which they passed and helped ignite the Industrial Revolution. At the same time they were dirty, busy, noisy and were built and worked on by a new and independent community of navigators and boatmen. Behind today's veneer of greenery, however, glimpses of this past can still be seen, reminders of this earlier age when canals were the motorways of their day and the working narrowboat the lorry!

The Origins of Canals

Artificial waterways have been built for thousands of years. Channels dug for irrigation can be found in the Ancient World, and the Romans were responsible for the Fossdyke between the Trent and the Witham at Lincoln, amongst other engineering marvels. The Chinese were probably the first to construct canals as we know them, and had devised locks to raise or lower their course over a thousand years ago. It was not until the reign of Elizabeth I that an artificial waterway with locks was built here, with the short Exeter Canal completed in 1566.

By this time fledgling industry, developing trade and increased prosperity were putting pressure on the still medieval road system and many looked at river transport as a more effective alternative. Rivers had always been used for carrying goods, but shallows, weirs and seasonal hazards made them unreliable. During the 17th and early 18th century, however, many were improved and navigation extended further upstream with new channels diverting traffic around difficult stretches and locks bypassing weirs, almost doubling the total mileage available to boats.

Rivers improved the situation for

FIG 1.2: FROGHALL, STAFFORDSHIRE: *The industrial surroundings of canals have usually been reclaimed today by nature. This example is the terminus of the Caldon Canal, once a busy centre where lime was unloaded, burnt in huge kilns and then transferred to the waiting narrowboats (top). Now it is a quiet tourist attraction in a beautiful wooded valley, with just the occasional glimpse of its industrial past (bottom).*

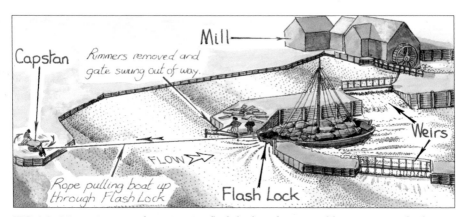

FIG 1.3: *Many rivers used a primitive flash lock so boats could move onto a higher or lower level. The craft were simply hauled or lowered through a gap accompanying a 'flash' of water. Later river navigations and canals used more advanced 'pound locks', which carefully raised the craft in a chamber created by gates at either end (see Fig 8.14).*

those industries and trades close at hand, but unfortunately one commodity in particular was more often than not too far away – coal. Artificial waterways, independent of rivers, began to be mooted by some as an answer to reaching areas further inland. The Sankey Brook Navigation reached the coalfields around St Helens, Lancashire in 1758, but it was the Third Duke of Bridgewater and the canal he built to serve his mines near Manchester that caught the public's imagination in the following decade. The Duke and his assistant John Gilbert turned to a millwright, James Brindley, to plan out the route from Worsley to Manchester, a waterway which proved a financial success and resulted in the price of coal plummeting in the city.

There was not an immediate rush, but a number of other dignitaries and industrialists saw the benefits and set about getting parliamentary approval for the building of canals, most notably linking the Trent, Mersey, Severn and the Thames in the form of a cross on a map of England. It was not until the last decade of the 18th century that the true financial potential of these first canals was appreciated and a mania for building them erupted, peaking in 1793 when Acts were passed for twenty separate canals. This pioneering spirit quickly waned in the wake of war with France and not all of those proposed were ever built, while others had to wait to be completed until Napoleon's downfall and an upturn in the economy in the 1820s.

Some of those built, like the Trent & Mersey or Aire & Calder, were financial successes and enjoyed a long life; others gave their promoters modest returns and hung on into the 20th century. Some set off on ambitious routes but were cut short when money

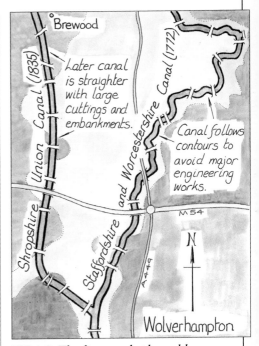

FIG 1.4: BRINDLEY'S MEMORIAL, STOKE-ON-TRENT: *James Brindley was the man of the moment and was sought by many promoters to survey and engineer their projects. He was born near Buxton, Derbyshire in 1716 and with little schooling learnt most of his skills as an apprentice millwright and then in his own business, set up in Leek, Staffordshire in 1742 (his restored mill here is open to the public). It was in this role that he developed techniques for building weirs, water channels and reservoirs, which made him an ideal choice to plan the first canals. He was involved in most of the early major projects, but he probably took on too much work and as a result gained a reputation for unreliability, ending up completing only a couple of canals before his untimely death in 1772.*

FIG 1.5: *The first canals planned by Brindley tended to follow the contours of the landscape to save on expensive and time consuming engineering works like cuttings and embankments. It was argued that these meandering routes could pass through more places to pick up trade – however, boatmen thought it meant they could be charged more as they paid tolls per mile! Later canals, especially major routes built after 1800, were more ambitious with a need to increase speed so were built straighter with massive earthworks and locks set in one block, which were quicker to work. This map, showing the junction between Brindley's meandering Staffordshire & Worcestershire Canal (right) and Telford's later more direct Shropshire Union Canal (left), illustrates this difference.*

FIG 1.6: *The English canals at their peak (around 1830) – narrow canals are marked in thin lines, wide canals in a broad line. Although it may appear as a national system it is important to realise that most canals were planned as short distance, independent waterways with mainly local traffic and daily boat services. Hence there were many different sizes of locks on narrow and wide canals, with different designs of boat to fit within them. Long distance journeys were increasingly undertaken but were restricted to narrowboats that could fit in all the different sized locks along their route.*

ran out, like the Ellesmere Canal (today the Llangollen Canal). A few, however, were complete failures, most notably the Cong Canal in Western Ireland, which when they let the water in at one end leaked so badly that it didn't reach the other, such a bad problem that it never actually opened!

This disaster highlights the main concern of canal builders – water supply. As canals end at a river or low point, water will always be drained down from their higher reaches whenever a lock is emptied. This means that there must be a reliable and sizeable water supply at the highest point of the route, its summit level, so it does not run dry. Many canals, especially later ones, were built 'broad' with wide locks so that larger river craft and barges could use them. However, Brindley's concern with water supply meant that he built his locks 'narrow' as a way of reducing the loss every time they were used. Nobody knows why he selected the size he did, approximately 72 ft long by 7 ft wide, but this physical constraint was the direct reason for the development of a unique craft, the narrowboat.

Early Boats

Various types of boats had developed that were unique to particular rivers in the centuries before the canals arrived. These used sails for power with a hinged mast to pass under bridges, but unlike sea-going vessels tended to be flat bottomed or a shallow V-shape with short or removable keels. If wind power was not available then these large, broad boats could be towed, 'bow hauled', by gangs of men. Before the canal age there were no purpose-built footpaths along rivers so obstacles had to be scrambled over and the bank could be littered with pitfalls – it was no place for a horse!

The First Narrowboats

The first narrowboats were probably based on the long, thin, open craft called 'starvationers', which were used to access the Duke of Bridgewater's mines at Worsley. These were simple flat-bottomed, straight-sided boats with pointed ends and it is likely that Brindley had their proportions in mind when deciding upon the size of locks on his canals. Partly due to this and to conserve water, he chose 72 ft long by 7 ft wide – dimensions which, in effect, created the narrowboat (up to 70 ft x 6½ ft). Many probably came from the same yards that built river craft, so

FIG 1.7: *A starvationer, the original craft used in the Duke of Bridgewater's mines at Worsley. They were around 36 ft x 4½ ft with oak side planking, elm bottoms and a square cross section. The boats were unpowered and dragged or pushed through the tunnels by men walking down the boat, using a pole and hook, or 'legging'. These are the craft that it is believed James Brindley had in mind when planning canals, which determined the sizes of narrowboats.*

some local and regional variations in their shape and construction continued.

The problem is that no examples survive from this early period of canals and illustrations are limited, most dating from after 1800. The boats would have had wooden hulls, with elm bottom planks and oak sides. Both the bow and stern would have been tapered with a tiller hinged at the rear. All these craft would have been towed, usually by horse. With no engines and no propellers to house, most of the space aboard was used for carrying goods. Decoration was probably limited as few lived on their boats at this time, with possibly just simple company logos and geometric patterns used to help identify a craft from a distance.

Many of these narrowboats were only designed for short local trips that were completed in a day so they may have had no cabin, or perhaps just a temporary canvas shelter. Boatmen could always stay overnight at an inn or with friends so there was often no need for a large cabin that would take away valuable cargo space (they were paid by tonnage carried so the more space the better the wage).

Some had small permanent cabins, especially those that were used for long distance travel. However, an important difference with early canals was that due to the relatively good wages to be earned most boatmen probably used their craft as lorry drivers do today. They kept their own houses on land and just worked away from home for the duration of the journey. Families on narrowboats were not common at first and only began to appear in numbers when trading became more competitive in the early 19th century.

Boatmen

Few of the canal companies who built the navigations took any interest in running the services along them. Their income came from charges for using the waterway, collected at toll houses or lock keepers' cottages along the route. They might build public wharfs, short cul-de-sac canals off the main line to serve major works (known as arms), and stables for horses, but only a few were responsible for their own fleets. Narrowboats were either run as a single craft, known as 'number ones', or by carrying companies of various

FIG 1.8: A NARROWBOAT c1800: *Canals were built for industry and the boats that plied their trade upon them in the late 18th century probably had little accommodation and only basic decoration (there are few pictures of boats from this period).*

FIG 1.9: *A horse with tackle towing a boat. Horses were usually the responsibility of the crew so stabling them at night was an important consideration and many canalside inns offered overnight accommodation for boaters and their animals.*

sizes. One of the largest of these was Pickford's, who ran a large fleet of craft before moving into railways and then the removal business by road.

The boatmen themselves came from many different backgrounds; some already worked the rivers and just moved over to these new easier to navigate waterways, others were involved in the building of the canal and simply stayed on to work it. In the early days both those who dug and worked on 'the cut' were referred to as 'navigators', it was only around the turn of the 19th century that boatmen were specifically thus named and those who built the canals were shortened to 'navvies'. The boatman might own his narrowboat or just crew it for a company. He would usually have one or two men with him to help with loading and locking and a boy who would look after the horse while it was towing.

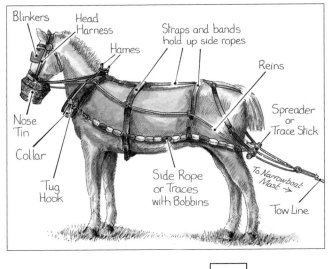

FIG 1.10: *Horses used were not of any particular breed and in some cases mules could be found towing boats. This illustration shows the tackle used which spread the load on the horse and protected its flanks with reins to guide it. The nose tin allowed the horse to feed without stopping.*

Towing and Legging

Unlike the river navigations, canals were purpose-built with a towpath often constructed from the spoil excavated during construction. Where the towpath changed sides a turnover bridge was provided, over which the horse could cross without having to disconnect the tow line. Another problem was when boats met, travelling in opposite directions. There were rules on who should give way and the priorities of different types of craft, but in general one boat went on the outside and either dropped or raised its

FIG 1.12: *Another solution that allowed the horse to continue towing was used on the Stratford upon Avon Canal where cast iron bridges were built with a narrow gap in the middle, which the rope could pass through without having to be disconnected. This example is from the Caldon Canal in Staffordshire (the railings are a recent addition).*

FIG 1.11: A TURNOVER BRIDGE:
Due to the right farmers had to use a bank for watering cattle, and also because of landownership and physical obstacles, the towpath often had to change sides. So that the horse would not have to disconnect from the boat it was towing, a turnover bridge, also known as a roving or changeline bridge, was provided. These usually had distinctive curving approaches on one side so that the horse could walk up and across, then back under the bridge on the other side without having to interrupt the towing.

line to allow the other boat and its horse to pass on the inside. Cotton was used for ropes with this in mind as it sinks in water.

When the boat approached a tunnel it would have to disconnect from the horse, which walked over the top of the hill to rejoin it on the other side (the paths they used can usually still be traced today). The un-powered boats had to make their own way through, usually by legging, although there were tricks of the trade and alternative methods in a number of locations. In the early days a single board was placed across the front of the boat and two men lay down on their backs at either end of it with their legs bent up against the tunnel wall. They simply 'walked'

Outer horse and boat drop their line so that inner craft can pass over the rope.

FIG 1.13: *A diagram of horses and boats passing each other. The boat at the bottom of the picture (outer) drops its line so that the craft at the top (inner) can pass by. The priorities varied from canal to canal but in general fast travelling fly and passenger boats had preference.*

along and slowly dragged the boat through with only a flickering candle for light, a much harder job than it sounds! It was only later that a few tunnels were provided with towing paths on one or both sides, although the horses were not too keen on the dark and dank conditions.

Despite competition from the turnpike roads, these new canals dominated the transportation of goods and stood at the forefront of technology for nearly seventy years. There were, however, limits to where canals could go and to solve this problem many companies built

FIG 1.14: LEGGING: *In most tunnels before the advent of powered craft the narrowboat had to be legged through by men resting upon a board. A problem with this system was that if someone fell off or slipped from one end then the man at the other end could topple into the canal! From around the 1850s two shorter boards (as shown here), which hooked onto a fixing on the front of the boat, were used so they were independent of each other should there be an accident.*

FIG 1.15: WHALEY BRIDGE, DERBYSHIRE: *Where a canal was not possible, as in this case across the Peak District, a tramway was built. Here at the end of the Peak Forest Canal a transhipment building was built to load goods to and from boats and waggons. The left-hand view shows the canal side, the right the road side (the far left door in this latter view was where the railway used to enter the building, the central one was the end of the canal).*

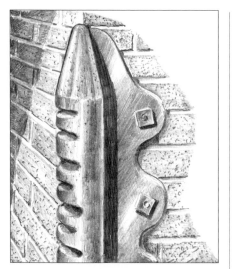

FIG 1.16: *Metal rubbing strips up the sides of bridges often retain the grooves cut into them by the ropes of horse-drawn boats.*

tramways to bring goods down to a waterside wharf or loading area. Others were built to connect separate lengths of canal, like the Lancaster Canal which ran out of money and had the final section completed by a tramway. These consisted of tracks with a horse pulling loaded waggons, by the end of the 18th century with L-shaped rails known as plateways.

Inadvertently, the canal companies in developing these new tramways were helping in their own downfall. In October 1829 a bright yellow train demonstrated just how far this new form of transport had come in such a short time, as Stephenson's *Rocket* won the Rainhill trials, helping ignite a mania for railways and bringing the end of the dominance of canals.

CHAPTER 2

The Slow Decline
1830–1945

FIG 2.1: *Despite the obvious advantage in speed that the trains had over the narrowboat, there were still important roles for canals to play and many remained as viable businesses right up until the Second World War. Cost cutting such as moving families onto boats also helped profits and created the colourful painted narrowboats we are familiar with today.*

Canals in the Railway Age

The arrival and dominance of railways over their water-bound competitors was sudden and rapid. Only a decade or so after the *Rocket* had won the Rainhill trials, more track was being laid in one year than there was total mileage of canals! Initially, boats benefited from supplying construction materials for the new railways but they quickly lost their most lucrative trade afterwards, with most being bought out by the new upstarts. The canals, however, were far from finished. Although a number were drained and their course used for a new railway, most were retained as viable businesses. Some were used by competing regional companies to take trade away from a neighbouring railway, while others continued as before, just with lower profits as they were left with cheaper goods per ton to carry.

Many canals remained important as towns and cities had grown up around them and the new railways could not reach the businesses that lined the waterways. Interchange basins were built further out where canals could unload goods picked up in these built-up areas and transfer them onto trains for longer journeys, keeping many of the urban waterways busy. Although

FIG 2.2: *It was a problem for railways to reach factories in built-up industrial centres so some erected interchange buildings with canals, enabling the goods to be brought by boat to the edge of town and then loaded onto trains. These worked in a similar fashion to the transhipment buildings (see fig 1.15) built by canal companies to transfer goods onto the tramways, which reached areas the canals could not!*

the railways offered speed, many companies continued to use the canal where they had their factory adjacent to it. There was no point in relocating or altering transport arrangements if once a pattern of deliveries had been established the canals could deliver reliably and at now much cheaper rates.

Some canals were run down slowly or had little spent on their maintenance by their new owners and there were a steady number of abandonments throughout this period, most in the 19th century being the less viable agricultural canals built in the mania without a sound financial footing! Those more important waterways and the few that remained independent, however, looked to improve their routes and speed up traffic. The Anderton Boat Lift in Cheshire, completed in 1875, and the Foxton Inclined Plane of 1901, near Market Harborough, were just two huge undertakings built to increase speed and improve connections.

A number of the early canals that meandered along contours were straightened out, new lengths of broad canals built and locks widened to take larger craft. The Manchester Ship Canal, cut in the 1890s, illustrated that waterways on a large scale which could handle sea-going vessels were still viable even if the early narrow canals of Brindley's age were less so. Despite all these efforts to keep trade flowing, by 1945 the future of the canal network looked bleak. Not only had many canalside industries closed in the interwar years, but what business the railways had not taken away, the new more versatile lorry was now about to.

FIG 2.3: *ANDERTON BOAT LIFT:*
This huge lift with two counter-balanced
chambers to carry boats connected the
Trent & Mersey Canal to the River
Weaver below and was opened in 1875.
It was a vast and complicated
undertaking, showing that companies
like those who owned these two
navigations still saw them as important
and viable businesses for the future even
in the middle of the Railway Age. This
wonder of the canal system has recently
been restored, with exhibitions and
parkland, at its site just outside
Northwich, Cheshire.

Changes to Narrowboats

Economic downturns in the early decades of the 19th century had already encouraged some boatmen to move their families on board to save the cost of maintaining a house on land and paying wages to a crew. With the drop in trade from the 1840s as railway competition began to bite, a larger number made the same move, resulting in changes to their narrowboats. A cabin at the rear with cleverly designed pull-out tables, beds and cupboards and, on many, a small additional space at the front in the bow were added,

although it took away some of the cargo-carrying space. As these were now homes, proud owners began decorating the exterior of their craft and the familiar brightly coloured scenes and patterns developed during the 19th century with specific regional, corporate and individual artists' variations on general themes (see Chapter 7).

Although these picturesque and snug boats seem idyllic today it must be remembered that families with children had to spend all their lives in these tiny spaces. Although they would have been outside for most of the day and the children would have slept under the canvas or in the fore cabin, the conditions could be appalling. A number of philanthropists, most notably George Smith of Coalville, campaigned for regulations to control the conditions on narrowboats, especially for children, resulting in the largely ineffective 1877 Canal Act and the more successful 1884 Act. Despite the provision of schools in some places the boating population, perhaps numbering around 20–30,000 at its peak, was largely uneducated and isolated, comprising a forgotten, shifting people who were little trusted or understood by society. Further legislation in the 1930s effected only minimal changes, although authorities did begin to carry out their duty of ensuring that some attended school.

Boating Families

Family-run boats were common in this period throughout the Midlands and North West, especially on the long distance routes; however, in areas like the South of England, South Wales and

Yorkshire where journeys were often shorter all-male crews still dominated.

Boating families came from a variety of backgrounds, but were nothing to do with gypsies. Many enjoyed a reasonable income even up to the mid 20th century. The canals could be an isolated world with close-knit communities and generations of the same family working 'the cut' (another name for the canals). Their vocabulary would usually reflect their area of origin, but with little opportunity for education they often mispronounced names. This was not a great problem as they usually renamed features along the waterways with their own titles after local personalities or features. For example, Hawkesbury Junction where the Oxford Canal meets the Coventry Canal is well known to boaters as 'Sutton Stop', named after its first lock keeper.

Those families who worked the longer routes had only a cabin rarely more than 10 ft long in which to shelter and store belongings while on the move. As was common with much of the population in this period, extended hours of work were followed by meals and entertainment away from the home, the same being true for many boating families who after cruising from 6 am until 6 pm or later would moor up and eat at canalside inns and pubs. The principal role for the cabin was as a shelter, sleeping quarters and somewhere to store and prepare basic meals.

While cruising, a simple cooked breakfast before setting off could be prepared on the stove inside and a cold meal for lunch en route meant the boat did not have to stop. Sunday was worked in the early 19th century until religious revival in the 1830s made it frowned upon, with many boating families taking the time for their one proper meal of the week, a steak or lobby (named after lobscouse, an old nautical term for stew). The solid fuel stove, which became a standard fitting in family boats from this period, was the centre point of the cabin. It provided heat for the room and acted as a cooker for meals. Water was stored in cans on the roof and moved about with dippers (metal bowls with handles) so it could be brought in to be boiled on the hot plate for tea or poured into bowls or tubs for washing. There were, however, no toilets fitted into the boats; a pan or bucket stored away may have been used by some, but others would just seize an opportunity as they cruised or use facilities on land when moored up at night. It was still common right up to the 1950s for waste to be poured directly into the canal!

Dress varied through the ages but men tended to wear jackets, waistcoats, full sleeved shirts and neckscarves, while women usually wore far more complex arrangements of long skirts, pinafores and blouses, with bonnets and shawls!

At busy times the boat would have been on the move for all the daylight hours so time for other domestic duties may have been limited to Sundays or periods when moored up awaiting work. This downtime also gave the proud families a chance to clean and polish their highly decorative cabins. Plates with ribbon threaded around the rim, brasses hung from leather straps, lace-edged curtains and painted scenes all contributed to give the cramped space a homely feel. Bed bugs were the worst problem for boating families and it was often necessary to fumigate cabins whilst in dock or when tied up along the towpath.

Powered Craft

Another major change to narrowboats during this period was the introduction of propulsion. Despite the widespread use of steam engines throughout industry and transport by the mid 19th century there had been little interest in fitting them to narrowboats. Experiments had been conducted with rear-mounted paddle steamers and a number were built for rivers where they performed well over shallow sections. On the tight spaces of a narrow canal and its locks this type was less suitable and when steam engines did begin to appear in the 1860s they were coupled to new screw propellers.

This in turn changed the shape of the hull. Rather than the gently sweeping rear of a horse-drawn boat onto which was hinged the tiller, propeller-powered craft had to have a pointed vertical end underwater so that water could be drawn over the prop with a counter

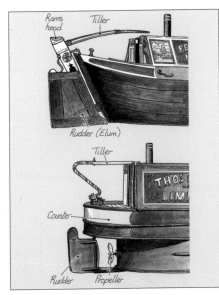

FIG 2.4: *The back of narrowboats changed in this period to suit boats fitted with propellers. The top example is that of a horse-drawn boat while the lower one is a motor narrowboat with the counter extended over the propeller. Boats (known as 'buttys') that were towed by the motorised craft had similar sterns to the horse-drawn boat.*

FIG 2.5: *Canal steam tugs were introduced in the mid 19th century and were used for various tasks. Many pulled boats through tunnels to speed up the passage of craft. These often had sprung wheels or other fenders to protect the tunnel walls and make steering easier. Space had to be allowed not only for the steam engine but also the coal to fuel it.*

FIG 2.6: *A famous sight around the canal network is the steam narrowboat 'President'. This beautifully restored working boat was built in 1909 and is now owned by the Black Country Museum, Dudley, where it is moored when not cruising.*

above it to keep the thrust created underwater. The man steering stood on top of this counter with the tiller hinged

FIG 2.7: *A restored motor boat (top) towing an unpowered tender, a butty (bottom).*

to the rear of it. Around 1911, diesel engines were introduced to narrowboats; the first were known as semi-diesels as they used paraffin or a light oil and were single cylinder engines (the most widely used were the Swedish Bolinder engines). In the interwar years proper diesels with twin or four cylinder engines appeared and most boats were built new with these or converted to use them (see Chapter 5). Horse-drawn boats were still common in the late 19th and early 20th century but by the Second World War they, along with the stables and towing path, were fast disappearing.

The introduction of engines meant that the cabin had to be elongated to accommodate them, taking away the valuable cargo space. However, steam and diesel engines were more powerful than a horse so 'buttys' were introduced. A butty was an unpowered tender the same size as the main boat, which could be towed and steered usually by the wife or children.

Hulls were also by this time beginning to be made with iron and a little later steel. Although metal hulls had been built as far back as 1787 at Coalbrookdale, it was not until the mid 19th century that they began to be produced commercially. They were part of a composite mixture at first, with elm planks retained for the flat bottom and iron, or later steel, riveted sides. In the early 20th century complete steel hulls were introduced and from the 1940s welding replaced riveting (see Chapter 4).

Day Boats

Although the traditional working boat we are familiar with today took shape in

FIG 2.8: *Day boats were used for just short journeys and often had no cabin as boatmen would stay on land after they had been moored up. They were a common sight around Birmingham where they were principally used for coal. Both ends were usually pointed so the rudder could be swapped from one end to the other without having to turn the boat around in often packed wharfs.*

this period there were still a large number of craft that were specifically used for short trips, usually of a day's duration or less. They might, for example, carry coal from mines that were a short distance from the works where it was required, with the loaded craft being left on site while the crew picked up an empty boat to take back. With this type of use there was little need for sleeping quarters so although their hulls were similar to those of the long distance narrowboat their cabins were small and in some cases nonexistent with little if any decoration. The greatest number of these seem to have been used in the Birmingham area.

Passenger Boats/ Flyboats

Initially the 1830s saw the blossoming of one particular type of boat, the flyboat. Passenger travel had started quite early in the canal age; despite the slow speeds of boats it was smoother and more

FIG 2.9: *The last horse-drawn flyboat to survive is 'Saturn', built in Chester in 1906. Its streamlined hull, system of swapping horses and a large crew of four men meant it could travel night and day to deliver goods faster. Earlier examples also carried passengers until railways took most of their trade away.*

FIG 2.10: *One of the biggest problems for canal companies was ice in winter. The narrow waterway could freeze up easily and various types of boats were designed to break it up to keep traffic moving. The left-hand example was horse-drawn, with men inside holding the top bar so they could rock the boat as they went along, cutting a channel. On the right is a later example of a motor-powered narrowboat with a heavy-duty angled bar fitted to the front; this didn't smash through the ice but pushed the boat up onto it, whereby its weight then broke it up.*

reliable than much of the road transport at the time. In the early 19th century there were experiments with new lighter boats, which could travel at twice the speed of conventional craft and yet create less of a wake (the wave created by a speeding boat, which damages the bank). These were introduced in the 1830s on the Forth & Clyde, Lancaster and a number of other canals, and had a canvas or permanent cabin to give passengers shelter. Although this traffic was lost to the railways over the following decades, flyboats continued to be provided for specialist and more speedy goods services. Not only could these boats travel faster, they also had priority over other traffic, which had to make way for them.

Committee Boats and Launches

Another type of craft familiar on rivers and occasionally found in a narrow form on canals was a launch. These were often luxuriously fitted out for the directors and board of the canal or railway company to cruise and inspect their waterway. Some were designed for river travel, others were narrowboats with an observation area at the fore.

The End is Nigh?

Canal and railway had worked alongside one another for much of the 19th century, despite a gradual decline in the former's freight carrying, but the 20th century and the arrival of the lorry had far more serious consequences. However, just as these four-wheeled menaces appeared over the horizon and the sun set on the less flexible narrowboat, a new dawn rose in the far distance. Only a few at first saw beauty in the still primarily industrialised and run down waterways, but these few turned into many and then a torrent as leisure boaters came to the rescue of canals.

CHAPTER 3

The Renaissance
1945–Today

FIG 3.1: BRAUNSTON, NORTHAMPTONSHIRE: *This famous junction on the canal network used to be busy with working boats loading and passing along the Grand Union or Oxford canals. Today it is even busier with pleasure boaters, boat festivals (the working boat festival is pictured here) and gongoozlers (a term coined by boaters for people who like to just watch narrowboats).*

Canals since 1945

The Second World War gave many canals a temporary boost in business, those boatmen who went off to fight being replaced by volunteers. Among their number were women, still a rare sight in a male dominated trade. At the end of hostilities the amount of traffic on the canals continued to decline. Most of what was left of the network was nationalised under the British Transport Commission, and the British Waterways

Board (BWB) was created in 1963. By then working boats were few and far between on the narrow canals, with most trade confined to the wider waterways like the Aire & Calder, the Manchester Ship Canal and the main rivers, which could handle larger boats.

However, help was at hand. Before the war a number of intrepid explorers had taken boats along these mysterious weeded and dilapidated waterways, often publishing their tales. By the 1950s and 1960s there was a new interest in canals and many took advantage of the relatively cheap holidays available to venture out along surprisingly beautiful and remote stretches of water, some only yards from busy towns and cities.

Groups were also forming to counter the steady decline and abandonment of canals. The network today only exists because of small, enthusiastic societies fighting to save canals under threat of closure and objecting to new roads or developments blocking those already shut. The Inland Waterways Association (IWA), formed just after the war by many of those early adventurers, played a key role in making the public aware of the plight of these waterways and established a National Rally to promote particular areas of the network, the first being at Market Harborough, Leicestershire in 1950.

FIG 3.2: *Rallies and festivals run by the Inland Waterways Association and local societies have been hugely successful. The National Rally held over the August Bank Holiday (this photo is from the IWA event at Wolverhampton in 2008) is a massive spectacle, great fun for all the family and a good introduction for those considering taking a canal holiday or buying a boat. Smaller local festivals, however, can get you closer to the craft, especially older working boats, which are often demonstrated.*

FIG 3.3: *From the 1960s an ever-increasing number of volunteers were prepared to get dirty and trudge around clearing rubbish and restoring the superstructure of canals (this photo is of work in the early 1970s in Manchester).*

FIG 3.4: *Another headache for waterways maintenance is dredging out the canal. All waterways silt up and if left unchecked this can cause blockages, especially in summer when levels are low. Dredgers come in all shapes and sizes. Most used on the narrow canals are flat, pontoon-type, steel boats with a small cabin and a digger arm that can excavate the canal bed. Other arms extend into the water to prevent the boat tipping over. These dredgers will either load the mud onto the adjacent bank or into a number of similar empty craft, which transport it off to another site where it is sometimes used for bank repair (often to fill in behind new steel piling).*

With the boom in the pleasure boat business, attention began to turn to restoration and the steady decline from the 1840s was slowly reversed. The first notable project was the reopening of the Lower Avon in 1963, followed shortly by the restoration of the Lower Stratford upon Avon Canal in the following year. By the 1970s most canals had groups and societies fighting to reopen them and with the aid of the IWA, the BWB and volunteers like the Waterways Recovery Group many succeeded.

The decline in working boats and increase in pleasure cruising brought changes to the canals themselves. Engines, ever since they were introduced in the late 19th century, have caused boats to create a greater wake behind them, resulting in damage to the often unprotected bank. This problem has been intensified by the larger number of craft that use the canals today. Concrete and stone have both been used in vulnerable areas but the most cost effective, if unattractive, solution is vertical steel sheet piling. The old wharfs, loading bays, docks and factory arms have mostly gone, but many were reused to form marinas, boatyards, moorings and boat clubs to suit the demands of the ever increasing pleasure boat business. Some of the buildings have also been converted into museums or pubs.

Pleasure Craft

When after the war a new generation of adventurers took to the waterways, most used either wooden river craft or converted old working boats with a large cabin covering the former cargo hold. Fibreglass cruisers suitable for canals and rivers became popular from the 1950s, especially as they required less maintenance compared with their wooden predecessors – apart from needing to be lifted out in winter to avoid damage from ice – and were relatively cheap to buy. Many a family, ours included, made their first steps onto the waterways with a Dawncraft,

Norman or Microplus GRP (glass reinforced plastic) cruiser!

Narrowboats that were purpose built for pleasure cruising began to be made from the late 1950s with all-steel hulls and either a GRP, wooden or metal cabin above. These were mainly for the new hire fleets, which became established around this time. As they were more expensive than the more flexible fibreglass cruiser, they remained in the minority until in the late 1970s when cheaper alternatives like Springer boats became available. These used thinner steel and a more mass-produced package to make an affordable step up from starter boats.

Engines had improved as well, with new quieter, water-cooled diesels

converted for marine use being widely available. These were more compact and could fit below the floor at the rear, creating precious additional room inside, and with new control systems the boat became much lighter to handle than the previous working boats. Today the canals are full of these steel leisure narrowboats, most built within the past twenty years, with a sprinkling of older ex-hire and original working boats. These craft are the ones you are likely to see, cruise on or buy today, and will be the focus of the remainder of the book.

Canals Today

When I was first introduced to boating as a boy in the 1970s the network was patchy in condition and size. Many canals had towpaths that had crumbled into the water, leaving the pedestrian stranded as the boat they were crewing disappeared over the horizon. Locks varied from stiff to practically immovable! Much fun could be had trying to push boats out after going aground as many canals silted up. My lasting memory, however, is of dirty, litter-strewn waterways creeping around the disused parts of towns and cities, which had turned their back on them.

The change today is remarkable. When we used to visit restoration society stalls at canal festivals we would throw in a contribution, have a chat and wish them luck. At best we thought they might open a lock or two – but the whole canal, never! Suddenly, however, under a flood of public interest, lottery and corporate funding and a change of attitude from local authorities, these ambitious schemes, which have ticked

FIG 3.5: *In the 1960s and 70s fibreglass boats dominated the canal system as they were much cheaper than steel narrowboats, had shallower depth (many canals were badly silted at the time) and more flexible as they could be towed. Marinas like Ladyline at Market Drayton on the Shropshire Union Canal were one of the biggest outlets for them.*

NARROWBOATS AND WATERWAYS MUSEUMS

There are excellent museums and visitor centres devoted to canals and narrowboats. During the spring and summer months they bustle with activity and make wonderful places for a day out.

Some of the larger ones are listed below and most have their own website.

The National Waterways Museum, Ellesmere Port. *Brings Britain's canal history to life.*

The National Waterways Museum, Gloucester. *Located in Gloucester Docks.*

The National Waterways Museum, Stoke Bruerne. *Not a large museum but packed with interest and close to locks and Blisworth Tunnel.*

London Canal Museum, at Kings Cross. *The only London museum of inland waterways.*

Black Country Living Museum, Dudley. *26 acres of living history.*

The Yorkshire Waterways Museum, Goole. *Celebrates the social and economic history of the canal port of Goole.*

Tooley's Boatyard at Banbury. *An historic working boatyard.*

The Canal Museum, Linlithgow. *Exhibits records, photographs and artefacts associated mainly with the Union Canal.*

The Museum of the Broads. *Uncovers the history of the Norfolk and Suffolk Broads.*

Bolton Steam Museum. *Restores old steam engines including some from boats.*

Shardlow Heritage Centre, based on the Trent & Mersey Canal. *Eighteenth-century canal port, with associated wharves and warehouses.*

The Kennet & Avon Canal Museum, Devizes, Wiltshire.

Ellesmere Boat Museum, Ellesmere Port, The Wirral.

BOAT SOCIETIES

Historic Narrow Boat Owners Club. *Encourages the preservation, restoration and use of old narrowboats.*

Wooden Canal Boat Society. *Dedicated to saving, restoring and using old wooden working boats.*

The Narrow Boat Trust. *A charity for restoring and preserving narrowboats.*

The Horseboating Society. *Promoting and preserving the heritage and skills of horseboating.*

FIG 3.6: ELLESMERE BOAT MUSEUM, THE WIRRAL: *A view of the old disused docks at Ellesmere, where the Shropshire Union Canal meets the Mersey. The same view today after restoration and although the buildings in the background are all modern the atmosphere of the old docks has not been completely lost. This is also the site of the National Boat Museum (there are additional museums at Stoke Bruerne and at Gloucester Docks), which is an essential visit for anyone interested in narrowboats and canals, with replica craft, unique exhibits and interactive features for the children.*

over for decades, have suddenly been completed.

Rather than turning their backs on canals, towns have welcomed the newly clean and vibrant waterway, seeing the advantages it can give rather than the costs incurred. Not only does the regeneration of a canalside area enhance the town or village, provide leisure facilities, opportunities for walkers, fishermen and boaters, it also attracts holidaymakers and brings revenue into the town, in some cases adding dramatically to the local economy. However, despite all the work that goes into creating these beautiful settings, the picture is incomplete without the colourful narrowboats!

SECTION II

NARROWBOATS
IN
DETAIL

CHAPTER 4

The Superstructure

FIG 4.1: *The imposing bow of a traditional narrowboat has elegant flowing lines that cut gracefully through the still canal waters. Yet what is it like beneath the surface, how are the boats built and what are the different types that can be seen?*

Narrowboats can be found today in all shapes and sizes from mighty old working boats to the most refined and colourful modern pleasure craft. Some are as short as 20 ft while most stretch upwards to 70 ft, although this figure is the maximum that will fit comfortably in most locks. There are exceptions, however, like the Leeds & Liverpool Canal and the Rochdale, which have shorter locks, so a length of around 57 ft is regarded as a sensible choice if you wish to cruise unobstructed through the system. Most boats today are around 6 ft 10 inches wide, which allows for the fact that lock walls, although 7 ft wide or more, bulge and sag with age, so a gap of a few inches is essential. Not only does the type and

FIG 4.2: *A modern steel narrowboat being craned into the canal, showing its flat base plate with no keel.*

size of boat vary but also finer details in the shape and profile, reflecting the fact that most narrowboats are still hand made by small local boatyards, each with their own designs and style. This individuality and regional variety is one of the delights of canals, yet most craft can be crudely grouped into a number of general types of narrowboat. In this section the hulls, cabins, engines, fittings and decoration of the working boats that survive and the pleasure craft that dominate the waterways today will be explained, while those exceptional craft that don't fall into any category can be better appreciated for their individuality.

THE HULL

Although the elegant lines of narrow-boats above water would imply a similar profile below, it may be surprising to know that the bottom of most boats is actually flat! In canals where boats are towed or powered there is no need for a keel, which is essential on sailing boats. More

important was maximising the cargo space so a box-shaped hull ensured a large hold, ease of loading and simplified construction, and in today's pleasure boats it creates more room for fittings (a few makes of boat have been built with a shallow V-shaped bottom, which makes mooring on shallow canals slightly easier). The sides are always at a steep angle to the bottom – known as hard chine – with internal angle brackets called knees to hold the sides and bottom in place on older boats and a framework of welded steel on modern craft.

Horse-drawn narrowboats and buttys

It is surprising just how many old working boats can still be found on the canals. Although the last finished haulage forty or fifty years ago many have been rescued and refurbished by enthusiasts. Others were converted to pleasure craft with the addition of a full-length cabin although the riveted hull or thick wooden planks are still a give-away of its origins. The oldest type of hull that can still be seen today is the one used on horse-drawn narrowboats and the similar later versions used as buttys (see Fig 2.7). Both of these had no engines, so not only was the majority of the hold free to house cargo but the stern post could be tapered off like the bow with just a large wooden rudder hinged on the back. This is usually a beautifully decorated feature with a broad post topped by a ram's head and an elegant bowing tiller handle so it could be steered from the cabin hatch (see Fig 2.7). The shaft was angled so that the weight of the rudder

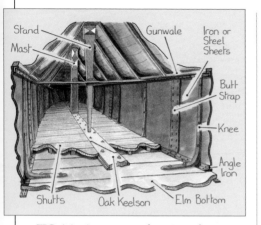

Stand
Mast
Gunwale
Iron or Steel Sheets
Butt Strap
Knee
Angle Iron
Shutts
Oak Keelson
Elm Bottom

FIG 4.3: *A cut-away drawing of a wooden working boat hull. This is a composite boat, which had metal sides fixed at the base to elm bottom planks.*

would always pull it back to centre if the tiller was released.

Motor narrowboats

Powered craft on narrow canals used propellers from their introduction in the 1860s. The problem was that they could not just be stuck on the rear of the existing type as the stern would not allow a good flow of water onto the blades and being so close to the surface the propeller would have lost grip (known as cavitation). To solve this problem narrowboats had a flat counter built over the top of the prop, the rounded or squared off end, seen above the waterline, from which the boat is steered (see Fig 2.4). Below the hull was tapered off so that water could run smoothly onto the prop. Some of the best hulls have an S-shape plan or a camber to the bottom plate, more complex steelwork

that could improve performance still further. Some horse-drawn boats were converted by adding a counter, others had their whole stern rebuilt.

Modern narrowboats have similar hulls to their working predecessors but generally have a shallow draught (the depth at which they sit in the water). Working boats tend to be around 3 ft

FIG 4.4: *Working boats had to pay tolls based on mileage and weight carried. The tonnage could be established in a boat-weighing machine, like this example at Stoke Bruerne, or by calculating the depth a boat sunk to when loaded and recording the tonnage on the side (lower picture). The heavier the load the deeper the boat sunk in the water (a rough rule on a 70 ft boat was about 1 inch down to every ton).*

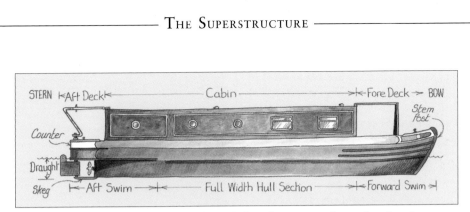

FIG 4.5: *A side view of a traditionally styled modern narrowboat, showing the sections of the hull known as the swim, which affect the performance of the boat through the water. At the rear or stern is the rudder held in place by the skeg and the propeller in front of it. Modern boats tend to use around a 17 inch diameter prop so that the depth from the waterline down to the bottom of the skeg is just under 2 ft (the draught). Older working boats and tugs had slower revving engines with large diameter props, hence they had to be deeper to accommodate this.*

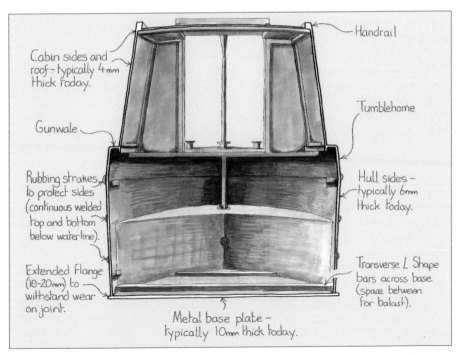

FIG 4.6: *A cross section through a modern steel narrowboat, showing some of the features and details that can be found on a good quality shell.*

whereas today's boats are just under 2 ft, a few even shallower. The advantage of a deep draught is that it is more stable but requires greater skill to steer to avoid running aground. This is less of a problem with modern boats but they will rock slightly more and very shallow draught boats are more susceptible to cross winds blowing them off course.

The shape and length of the swim – the section forward and aft from where the width narrows and tapers to the stern post and stem post underwater – is crucial to how well the boat will pass through water, the wake it will create and its manoeuvrability. Short, stubby swims will probably result in poor manoeuvrability, and this is an accepted downside of trying to fit the maximum width and cabin size onto a 30 ft or 40 ft boat. Longer craft or those that put hull shape before accommodation can have longer, gently tapering swims, which can give better performance.

The sides of most hulls rise up at a slight outward angle until just below the gunwale they angle back in again, giving them greater strength to resist knocks, aided by side rubbing strakes. Some have the sides formed by having the steel pressed into the finished shape, others are made up from vertical sheets simply welded into place. The latter is a cheaper method of construction but, depending on the thickness of material and clamping whilst welding, can be prone to leaving unsightly wavy sides.

Tugs

Tugs used for pulling craft through tunnels and other heavy duty work had larger diameter propellers and a slow

FIG 4.7: *A couple of restored tugs. They were a type used on the Birmingham Canal Navigations and had a large cabin covering two-thirds of the length from the back. This format makes it popular with many pleasure cruisers today who want a traditional form of boat without losing too much convenience. The hundreds of miles of canals that made up the BCN were consistently deep so these craft, with only the top foot or so of the hull showing above the waterline, could tow a number of boats at a time.*

turning, high torque engine to give them more grip in the water. This was further enhanced by the deeper hull, which was necessary to house the larger prop. These boats generally sat low in the water as a result, whereas working boats would only do so when fully laden with cargo.

CONSTRUCTION
Wooden hulls
Wood was virtually the exclusive material for the hulls of narrowboats for the first hundred years of canals and some were still being built in this way even up to the 1930s. These craft generally had oak plank sides and elm

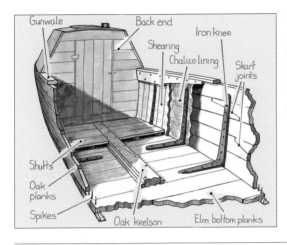

FIG 4.8: *A section through a horse-drawn wooden narrowboat, showing the layers and parts that went into its construction (there may have been variations on these depending on the boatyard).*

for the flat bottom (elm can survive being permanently wet for centuries – medieval bridges have been found with elm beams still intact in their foundations). The base planks were laid across the width of the boat with a central keelson running up the length of the hull and angled metal and wooden knees holding the sides and bottom together. The long side planks were laid flush on top of each other after being run through a steam box to help bend them into the required shape. The joints

FIG 4.9: *In order to bend the planks of wood into shape they were run through a steam box as in this example at the Black Country Museum. The pipe in the top came from a boiler.*

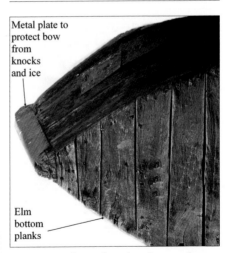

Metal plate to protect bow from knocks and ice

Elm bottom planks

FIG 4.10: *The underside of a wooden hull, showing the elm planks across the bottom and a metal plate over the stem post to protect it, principally from ice.*

between the ends could be butted up but angled scarf joints were often used as this gives greater strength to resist the wood trying to regain its former shape. When complete, an oakum rope was forced into the gaps – caulking – to help make the hull watertight. Some boats had metal sheets fixed around vulnerable parts of the hull to protect the wood against damage from ice.

Composite and metal hulls
The move to metal hulls was gradual and a popular intermediate step, which

was used right up until the end of the working boat era, was a composite hull. These had metal sides, first iron and later steel, with a wooden base as the elm planks used were easier to replace. All-metal hulls were common by the 1930s, by which time steel was widely used. Before the Second World War these were made from sheets that were overlapped and riveted to form the structure, but by the 1950s welding had become the usual way of joining the sheets together.

Modern steel hulls
Narrowboats produced over the past twenty or thirty years for the private pleasure cruising market now dominate the waterways. Although each boat-yard will have its own preferences for specification and details in the construction, most are built along similar lines.

The steel used is listed in millimetre thickness, and quoted with the base plate/sides/cabin thicknesses in the

FIG 4.11: *A number of narrowboats were actually built from reinforced concrete during the Second World War! This surviving example had a cracked bow (lower picture) exposing the metal reinforcing rods.*

FIG 4.12: *Steel and iron boats were riveted together prior to the Second World War. After this, welding became the norm in constructing metal boats.*

FIG 4.13: *The early stages of constructing a modern steel narrowboat (left) with the sides being cut to bend in and form the swim up to the prop. A later stage with the shell complete (right) showing the steel bars which reinforce the metal shell.*

FIG 4.14: *Although boats were purpose built for pleasure cruising back in the 1950s, it was not until the late 1970s that the market for privately owned, all-steel narrowboats really took off. One of the pioneering mass-produced makes was Springer, who by using thinner plate and cost cutting techniques dramatically reduced the price of these craft. To achieve this, the hull was formed out of large sheets, which were folded to create the cross-section shape and joined together at the bottom of a shallow V-shape. This gave the boats a distinctive appearance with exposed welds, stubby moustached bows (above left) and a slightly vulnerable corner where the hull had been folded. Most of these used a thinner steel; this is not necessarily a problem if it is regularly maintained but the point where the sides are folded to make the bottom stretched the outer surface and is potentially a weak point. Around the same time Hancock and Lanes began mass-producing a hull with a more traditional profile, thicker steel and a better finish. These were more expensive but were still cheaper than much of what went before, and set the standard for the modern pleasure narrowboat.*

specification. A common combination found today on most good quality boats today is 10/6/4. The extra thick 10 mm steel bottom is not there just to be more resistant to corrosion (the hull is actually more vulnerable at the waterline due to the air, oxygen and water mix) but it is used as built-in ballast. It also makes a tougher protruding edge at the join with the side plates where it sticks out around 10 mm so that impacts and corrosion wear down the overlap and not the weld.

The side sections are welded onto the base plate on both the inner and outer edge to meet modern regulations. The real skill is in forming the elegant swim at the bow with the gently curving stem post and the tapering shape at the stern up to the prop. Steel rubbing strips are then welded onto the hull with a continuous weld along the top edge and just spots below, although sections that are submersed should be continuously welded top and bottom. Angled steel bars are welded to the interior of the shell to strengthen parts of the hull and cabin and to provide fixings for the interior fittings.

Despite the weight provided by the base plate, fittings, engine and tanks, ballast is always needed to get the boat sitting neatly in the water and to stabilise the hull to reduce rocking. The usual method is to lay concrete paving slabs into the spaces between the cross members under the floorboards, leaving a small air gap so any moisture that gets in can evaporate. Gravel, concrete poured in and bricks can also be used – grey/blue engineering bricks are particularly good as they are very dense and moisture resistant (a problem with gravel and concrete is that they can trap moisture which never evaporates).

FIG 4.15: *Anodes: Steel's weakness is corrosion and painting the hull (blacking) needs to be done regularly to maintain it. The principal problem is the damage caused by the slightly acidic nature of canal water and one of the best ways of reducing the problem is to fit anodes. On the steel hull the slight difference in metal composition between one sheet and another creates the effect that the metal, which is more susceptible to corrosion, loses material. Over the years, this reduces the thickness of parts of the hull. This can be remedied by welding to the hull a metal lozenge that is chemically designed to erode in the water before the steel and hence this is worn away rather than the boat. These are also known as 'sacrificial' anodes and need to be replaced when they are worn, every three to four years depending on the water quality.*

FIG 4.16: *Bow fenders made from decoratively tied rope around a rubber core are not only a picturesque element but also important protection on the stem post, more for the things the boat will hit – like lock gates – rather than the hull itself (they are compulsory as part of the British Waterways safety check). Fenders down the sides are essential on fibreglass boats but are less common on steel narrowboats as rubbing strips will prevent any major damage. Decorative fenders, lengths of rope with a rubber sleeve or even tyres are chosen by some to cut down on the repainting as the sides quickly become scraped, especially when moored.*

THE CABIN AND HOLD

Working boats

The hold of a working boat was usually panelled out in wood with a framework of uprights and planks to support a tarpaulin over the top. At the front of this was a vertical triangular wooden support called the cratch. This covered the end of the hold (mirroring the front of the cabin at the other end) and held up the start of the line of planks along the top of the hold, which the crew could walk along. Vertical posts and the main mast on craft that were towed supported the planks with a cabin block at the far end. The mast was telescopic, with a thinner inner post that could be raised or lowered accordingly and from which the rope to the horse or motor boat was connected.

The deeper hull on a working boat meant that the cabin could be lower, with a sliding hatch cover that could be pushed back to get in and out without banging heads on the low roof (although the step down into the cabin was large and sudden). The cabin could be made of wood or riveted metal sheets, often with no windows fitted, so that every inch of interior wall space could be used for fittings. On a horse-drawn boat or butty the cabin was rather squat but on powered working boats it was taller with near vertical sides, in order to house the engine with enough space around it to work and to accommodate the drive shaft which ran under the cabin floor.

Modern narrowboats

In the early days of pleasure cruising, full-length cabins added to old working boats or fitted on new steel hulls were not only produced in metal but also wood and fibreglass! These last two can give problems with leakage, poor insulation and can be damaged when jumped on. They should be treated warily if considering as a purchase.

Modern narrowboat cabins are built with a steel shell, reinforced by longitudinal and vertical bars, which also allow for insulation to be fitted between them. Cabin sides angle in

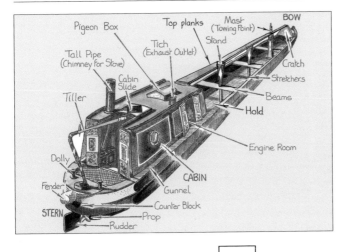

FIG 4.17: *A traditional working boat with labels of parts of the cabin and hold.*

FIG 4.18: *The finished steel shell of the cabin is lined with insulation, in this case spray on foam (top), which is afterwards covered by a thin ply sheet (bottom).*

to allow water to drain off. On many cruiser types they are a round rail raised up on supports, easier to hold but less traditional.

One of the most distinctive differences between types of pleasure craft today is the choice available for the style of stern to suit how they wish to cruise. Many hire boats and early private boats have a cruiser end on which the cabin is reduced in size to allow for a large open rear with rails around and seats so a group of people are able to sit with the driver. This more communal arrangement meant the engine is accessed from the outside under the floor that the crew stand on. A traditional end has become the most popular over the past twenty years; this replicates the working boat arrangement with just a short rounded stern of three to four feet and the maximum length of cabin. In this arrangement the engine is partly housed in the rear of the cabin. A modern compromise, which has gained popularity, has the external appearance of a traditional boat with a short end but has seating within the rear of the open end of the cabin.

slightly (the term is 'tumblehome'), not so much as to feel tight inside but not too vertical as to look ungainly and hit narrow bridges. The roof is slightly curved upwards (with a camber of a few inches or so like a road surface) to give it strength for standing on and running rain off. Handrails are essential for grip while walking along the gunwales and for keeping accessories from rolling into the canal. On traditional-style craft they tend to be square-boxed steel with small gaps

FIG 4.19: *The three types of stern that can be found on modern narrowboats. Traditional (left), cruiser (middle) and composite, semi trad (right).*

CHAPTER 5

The Engine

FIG 5.1: *'President', one of a series of Fellows, Morton and Clayton narrowboats, was fitted with a compound steam engine. Although today it has a different type the sight of this motor boat and its butty appearing along the canal is none the less impressive.*

Steam Engines

Power came late to narrowboats compared with other forms of craft, with compact steam engines being fitted by a number of companies only in the second half of the 19th century, long after their use in paddle steamers and ships. These early engines and their boilers took up a large space, being sited immediately forward of the cabin and also requiring storage for coal. Although they reduced the cargo tonnage by around a quarter they were powerful enough to pull a separate unpowered butty, which could increase the total carried. Horse-drawn narrowboats, however, remained in widespread use during this period.

Within the engine room there would have been the boiler with a pump supplying water from the canal into it and a coal or coke fire below. One of the crew would have stayed most of the time here, keeping the fire going, monitoring and controlling the engine. In the engine's simplest form there was a single cylinder, mounted vertically, pushing down the piston rod, which turned the crank at the bottom. This was fixed to the prop shaft, which ran under the cabin and out to the propeller, which could turn forward and backwards depending on which way the flywheel was turned.

Fellows, Morton and Clayton, one of the largest and most famous canal carrying companies, fitted more advanced compound steam engines to 31 of their craft from 1889, and continued to use them for around 40 years. In these the steam was drawn into a high pressure cylinder and then an additional low pressure vessel alongside before being exhausted into a condenser (this retained some of the water, which was then reused in the

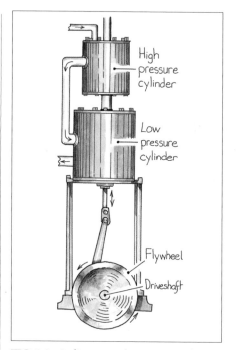

FIG 5.3: *A diagram of a compound engine with tandem mounted cylinders, which act together to turn the driveshaft below.*

boiler). These two cylinders, acting together, made for a more powerful and efficient engine (see Fig 5.3).

Hot Bulb or Semi Diesel Engines

Internal combustion engines, which developed in the last decades of the 19th century, were more compact, efficient and required less maintenance compared with steam engines. As they did not have boilers it freed up more room for cargo, which was just one of the reasons why they were adopted by

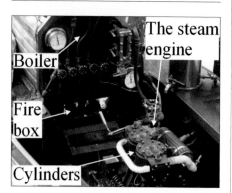

FIG 5.2: *A compact steam engine fitted to a launch. It shows the basic components of marine steam engines: the boiler supplying steam to the cylinders, which power a vertical piston turning via a crank the driveshaft below.*

FIG 5.4: BOLINDER ENGINE: *These Swedish engines were popular for narrowboat fittings. Bolinder had 80% of the global market in marine hot bulb engines in the 1920s and these were used in working boats well into the 1950s. The company is now part of the Volvo group after merging with Munktell.*

narrowboat owners more readily than steam had been, with the first being fitted in 1911. These were made by a legendary name on the canals, Bolinder, a Swedish company who dominated the narrowboat engine market in these early days.

These first examples were hot bulb oil engines, usually referred to today as semi diesels. They worked slightly differently from later types. They have one vertical cylinder with a piston connected by a rod and crank to the flywheel. Attached to the cylinder is the hot bulb, a chamber which is heated by an external blow lamp, into which is sprayed oil on the first down stroke, which vaporises due to the heat. At the same time fresh air is drawn in and when the piston makes its up stroke it becomes compressed and its temperature rises so that as it mixes with the vaporised oil they ignite, forcing the piston down again (the power stroke).

To start the engine, boatmen had to pre-heat the hot bulb with the blow lamp for up to five minutes (longer in extremely cold conditions) and then kick start the flywheel until its momentum could keep the engine running through the non-power parts of the cycle (see Fig 5.5). This type of engine, although not as powerful as

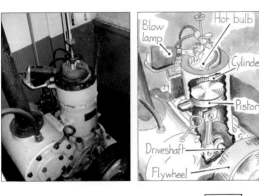

FIG 5.5: *Photo of a hot bulb Bolinder engine with a labelled drawing featuring a cut-away that shows inside the cylinder. Because these engines used both the heat of the hot bulb and that created by the compression of the air in the top of the cylinder to create ignition, they are known as semi diesels today, as a diesel uses just compression to ignite the fuel.*

contemporary diesel engines, was very simple, reliable and safe, and as the fuel is mechanically injected there is no electric system. It could also be operated on a variety of cheaper oils like paraffin, due to the method of ignition, and could be left to run for hours without attention.

Diesels

Shortly after the hot bulb type had been developed, Rudolf Diesel was perfecting his own internal combustion engine. Although similar to the hot bulb type, it injected the fuel into the cylinder as the air was being compressed by the piston, with no additional heating. A problem with the original diesel engine was that the fuel was injected by compressed air in order to force it into the already highly compressed air in the cylinder. This system limited its speed and it took the introduction of a modified pump and injector system by Robert Bosch before high speeds became possible. By 1910 diesel engines had been developed to become far more efficient and powerful with far greater rpm. At the same time there had been very little advance made with the hot bulb engine and its limited speed and power range.

By the 1930s diesel engines began to be fitted into narrowboats. In 1934 the Grand Union Canal Carrying Company Ltd ordered a new fleet into which were fitted Russell Newbury DM2 diesel engines. After the initial 38 were supplied they were unable to keep up with demand and the engines were built under licence by the National Oil Engine Company and known as the 2DM. Other engines that found their way onto narrowboats around this time included Lister JP2s, Kelvin K2s and Gardeners, most of these continuing in production after the Second World War along with new makes like Petter, Ruston & Hornsby and Armstrong Siddeley. These traditional, vintage or real diesels can still be found powering boats today and there is a lively market for reconditioned units to be fitted into new or old craft.

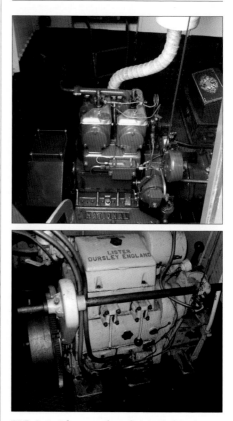

FIG 5.6: *Photos of traditional diesels made by National and Lister.*

Modern Diesels

Most narrowboats today will have more modern, compact and quieter diesels (the latter not being an advantage to those traditionalists who prefer the gentle thump of an old single cylinder). These will originally have been designed for generators, pumps or for light industrial use, and tend to be easier to maintain than those built for the more compact space and fast revving demands of a modern car. Some come from companies like Lister, Perkins, old BMCs and Ford but in recent decades an increasing number are Japanese from makers such as Mitsubishi, Yanmar and Kubota. Most of these need adapting for marine use and notable marinisers of engines suitable for narrowboats include Vetus, Isuzu, Shire, and Beta Marine. One of the main things which has to be done is fitting a 2:1 or sometimes 3:1 reduction gearbox as the propellers usually turn at 100–800 rpm and not the 500–2,000 rpm of the engine (larger propellers turn at slower speeds). The size and pitch of the propeller blades are matched to suit the appropriate gearbox.

These diesel engines can be air or water cooled, the former with ducts in and out of the hull, the latter either with water filtered out from the canal or from a thin cooling tank welded onto the skin of the boat. Exhausts can be fed out of the side or rear of the hull or through a chimney in the roof. The prop shaft is connected to the gearbox (which is bolted onto the engine) via a thrust plate, which absorbs shocks such as when the propeller hits something in the canal. The prop shaft will often run through a flexible coupling which protects the bearing from the vibrations of the engine where it passes through the hull. More expensive versions can also permit the engine to be mounted off-centre if required. Nearly all modern narrowboats will use a single lever control for the engine. Most are in neutral when the lever is vertical. Moving it towards the front increases the speed going forward and pulling it back does likewise in reverse (in effect, it is a gear stick and accelerator in one). Longer boats of 60–70 ft in length can be tricky to manoeuvre so some have a horizontal tube across the front underwater into which is fitted a bow thruster, a simple propeller powered by an electric motor controlled by a switch at the stern.

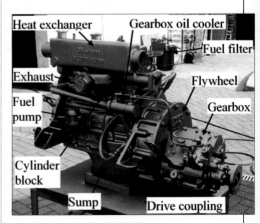

FIG 5.7: *A modern diesel engine prior to fitting in a narrowboat, with labels of some of its key parts. On this engine, water is pumped in from the canal and piped to the heat exchanger on the top where it cools the engine's water system (as a radiator does on a car).*

Propellers and Rudders

Although the boat builder or engine mariniser will recommend a particular propeller to suit the engine used, many boat owners with experience will look to change this. The diameter of the prop and the angle of pitch of the blades will affect the performance of the boat and they are also available in either right or left hand operation, depending on which way your prop shaft turns.

The boat is steered by a rudder fitted to the rear of the counter. On old horse-drawn working boats this was a huge wooden structure with an elegantly curved tiller handle and a couple of iron pintles that fitted into loops on the back and sometimes the front of the boat (so it could be towed either way round). The motor, however, had a figure-of-seven-shaped tiller similar to modern narrowboats, with a steel rudder below. This usually sits in a cup at the bottom fixed to the skeg (a horizontal bar which runs from under the propeller) and through a ball bearing casting bolted to the deck above.

Ancillary Parts

The engine will either be under the floorboards at the back of a cruiser-end narrowboat or within the end of the cabin, partly under steps or fully exposed, in a purpose-built space or room. Apart from the diesel there will also be a bilge pump as even in the most watertight craft there will always be a build up of damp (from condensation and spillage as much as any leak). The prop shaft needs grease to be

FIG 5.9: *A rudder from a horse-drawn boat or butty (the bowing tiller that slotted in at the top is not fitted here). The rudder or elum was hung at a slight angle to the back of the boat so it always centred itself if released.*

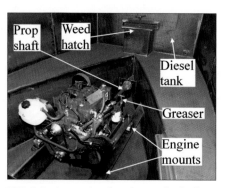

Prop shaft | Weed hatch | Diesel tank | Greaser | Engine mounts

FIG 5.8: *An engine fitted into the hull, with labels of parts.*

forced into the fitting around the steel boss, which is welded against the hull in order to keep it watertight. A metal grease cylinder with a handle is regularly turned to screw down the grease.

Canals are cleaner today than when I began boating but there is still rubbish, especially plastic bags, and sometimes heavy weed which can get tangled around the prop (juddering, noise or a bubbly trail to one side behind the boat is often a clue that something is wrapped around it). At the rear of the compartment above the prop is a weed hatch, held in place by a screw clamp, which can be unscrewed once the engine is turned off and the prop can be cleaned by hand. I never had a problem

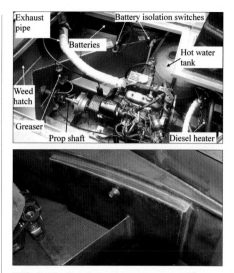

FIG 5.10: *The rudder and tiller on a modern narrowboat with a cruiser-style back. The rudder is held in place by a cup fitted on the skeg and a ball bearing ring on top of the counter.*

FIG 5.11: *Engine compartment with labels of ancillary parts (top). The hot water tank and diesel heater are often fitted elsewhere on larger narrowboats. The engine in this example is cooled by a skin tank (bottom), which is fitted to the side of the swim to chill the water.*

FIG 5.12: *A brass flame trap, which allows air to escape but prevents flames getting in or out of the diesel tank below. This example runs through the centre of a dolly, a pair of which are usually fitted at the rear of traditional-style boats for the mooring ropes.*

FIG 5.13: *Fitted above the cabin roof are chimneys, either short or tall and used for the exhaust above an engine room on traditional-style boats or at the rear above the stove. On modern boats they are usually fitted partly for decorative purposes and to vent either a diesel or solid fuel stove. They fit over a cast base plate so they can simply be lifted off when going under a low bridge and for security when moored. They are painted gloss black with brass bands at the top and traditionally had decorative horse brasses on a vertical leather band hanging from them.*

with this awkward procedure until someone told me that a pike was seen cruising along this particular stretch and my arm was quickly withdrawn!

The diesel is filled up through a brass screw cap along the gunwale, usually above the tank. This is typically fitted in a welded steel form in the engine compartment. There will be a small breather hole set high up with a brass flame trap, so that air can get in but no flame can enter or exit.

FIG 5.14: *A pigeon box. To vent the engine room on motor working boats a hole was cut in the roof and a box with lifting flaps either side was put over it. Later examples also had small portholes fitted to increase the light below. These were removable and were decorated with roses.*

CHAPTER 6

The Cabin

FIG 6.1: *The traditional working narrowboat cabin managed to fit into a space rarely more than 10 ft long a cooker, table, seating and a double bed. Today's boat builders may have a much larger space yet still require the same ingenious built-in furniture and ergonomic skills to fit in all the demands of modern life within strict safety regulations!*

Traditional Working Boat Cabins

Cabins on working boats varied from a tiny space at the rear of dayboats, designed just to give enough room for a stove for the crew to make a brew, to a larger – though rarely more than 10 ft – space to house a family. As regulations began to be enforced under the 1884 Canal Act a small front cabin in place of the foredeck was often built to create some more sleeping room, to comply with the law without reducing the valuable cargo space.

The layout of the working narrowboat cabin was remarkably similar on all makes, restricted as it was by the space available and the essentials required by the boat family. The cabin was accessed through a pair of hinged doors at the rear, with a door at the other end to reach the engine room on a motor narrowboat. On the left would have been a recess for a stove, a solid fuel type, usually with a hotplate and oven, which allowed basic cooking tasks to be carried out and provided heat for the compact living space. Next was a built-in cupboard with a top hinged panel, which when lowered became a table with open shelving in the recess behind for foodstuffs. Below this was a drawer and a cupboard for pots and pans. The last part of the left side was another shallow built-in cupboard, again with a drop-down door, which bridged the gap between this and the

FIG 6.2: *The cabins on motor narrowboats (top) are taller than those on a butty (middle) to allow for the propshaft to run below and for headroom in the engine room, which adjoins it. Many boats after the 1880s had small forecabins fitted (bottom) to increase accommodation space in line with changes in the law (see Chapter 2).*

FIG 6.3: *A cut-away drawing of the interior of a working motor narrowboat with labels of parts. The pull-down table was hinged at the bottom as was the bed beyond it, which dropped down onto the seat on the other side to use the full width of the boat.*

FIG 6.5: *Buckets to store water for use for drinking (usually boiled to make tea rather than drunk straight) and a pan to collect water out of the canal or river were kept on the cabin roof. They were usually richly decorated with roses and often displayed the name of the boat or its owner.*

FIG 6.4: *The interior of a working narrowboat cabin; the top picture is looking down the left-hand side with the stove and table, the bottom one shows the seating on the right-hand side.*

the rear door to keep books and receipts for the boatmen to have close at hand when paying tolls etc. Lighting was provided by candle or lamp, with electric lights only appearing on some later boats. Gas was rare as heat was provided by the solid fuel stove, and water was stored in a bucket on the roof and dispensed inside as required.

Modern Narrowboat Cabins

Pleasure boats today have no such rudimentary services; the modern cabin would have seemed like a palace to the working boat family. Running water, electricity and gas are provided on most so that, if wished, all the luxuries you would expect at home can be transferred to the boat. Flat screen TVs, dishwashers, showers and computers

seat on the opposite side to make a bed across the width of the boat.

The right side as you enter the cabin was fitted out with built-in seating that could be used as a bed at night. A small drawer was fitted in the ceiling close to

REGULATIONS

There are two principal regulations that control the standard of build and safety of modern narrowboats. British Waterways' Boat Safety Standards were first introduced to cover hire boats and then later in 1995 were applied to all, becoming mandatory in 1998. The regulations are designed to ensure that all craft on their waters are safe and they pay particular attention to the gas, electricity and diesel services in narrowboats. In the early years they were considered over the top and were somewhat watered down after being challenged in court by a boat-owning barrister! Today the regulations are more stable and require the owner to arrange an inspection every four years, without which a British Waterways licence (compulsory to cruise the waterways) cannot be obtained.

The European Recreational Craft Directive was made mandatory in 1998 and concentrates on the standards of construction and sea worthiness of all recreational craft up to 24 m long (approx 75 ft). Any boat that is constructed for sale must be certified as complying, except those to be cruised for at least five years by the builder himself. There are many exceptions and problems with the scheme, intensified by the vast number of different types of craft covered. As it applies to boat builders it should not affect most people who intend to buy or hire, other than the need to check that the craft has a CE mark (ensuring conformity to regulations) and an owner's manual.

FIG 6.6: *Gas cylinders are located in a secure metal box, which is usually fitted at the rear as in this case or in the foredeck.*

can all be found on modern narrowboats. What is different, however, is the way the utilities are supplied and sometimes the type of device you can use.

Heating and Gas

'Is it cold in winter?' is one of the most frequently asked questions of anyone living on a boat. It comes as a surprise to most to find the opposite is true. When visiting my parents with their narrowboat covered in snow I would usually find doors wide open to let the heat out! This is due to most modern boats having good insulation all around the cabin, a relatively small space to heat (with a low ceiling) and the fact that the lower half of the craft is surrounded by water rather than sub zero winds.

The heat itself can be provided by a gas boiler, a diesel heater or a solid fuel stove. The wood or coal burning stove is an attractive feature where space permits – usually in the forward dining or lounge

FIG 6.7: *Solid fuel freestanding stoves are a popular way of providing heat. Some are linked into a series of radiators to further distribute the heat.*

area with a chimney above. These can be independent or with a back boiler to feed either a complete central heating system or just one or two radiators as a back up to the main supply. Diesel heaters can either be compact forced-air types, which can be housed in the engine compartment, or larger gravity-fed boilers, which are simpler but being larger need a bit more thought as to siting. These both use fuel from the engine's tank or a separate one dedicated for central heating, with diesel being safer and less of a problem with regards to modern regulations than gas.

Gas boilers were popular in the past for heating but nowadays only those with a balanced flue are permitted on new craft, leaving builders with a very limited choice. These are supplied from bottles stored in metal lockable containers, usually in the foredeck and occasionally at the rear (there are tighter regulations with running gas pipes through engine compartments so it is often easier to site them at the front). Diesel and gas heaters are connected into a series of radiators, just as at home, and also into more compact finrads (lengths of pipe with short metal fins) or hot air blowers, which can be sited in tight spaces. The gas cylinders can also provide a supply for the cooker and a fridge.

Hot and Cold Water

Running hot water for the sink and bathroom was traditionally supplied by a wall-mounted gas heater and they can still be used where originally fitted in an older pre-regulation-dated boat. However, the demand for a balanced flue has meant that modern narrowboats usually have a calorifier, a hot water tank which is heated by coiled pipes fed with hot water from the engine's cooling system and in many from a separate heater as well. This means that even in summer when the central heating is off, a period of time with the engine running will still create a tank of hot water for washing.

The cold water to supply the boiler, calorifier, sink and bathroom is stored in a tank, often under the foredeck, its weight helping to ballast the front of the boat. It is usually fitted as part of the shell, with a welded steel panel across the bow and the inside painted with a special bitumen to prevent corrosion. On some more luxurious boats a stainless steel or plastic tank can be fitted within this space. Depending on the tank and the time that water has been left in it you can find that the drinking water has a strange taste, and many use bottled water or a filter jug. As the tank is level with or below the taps and showers there is no gravity to make the water flow as there is in a house. A water pump is therefore fitted, which tends to make a distinctive whirring noise when a tap or the shower is turned on.

Waste water from the sink, basin and shower (or bath in some cases) has nowhere else to go except straight out into the canal. It is worth bearing this in mind as habits from home like pouring bleach or forcing food waste down the sink can have nasty effects on the water outside! The same is true of those larger boats that have a washing machine and dishwasher fitted; although modern versions of these are efficient with water they may still throw out two or three watering cans worth of diluted detergent.

Electrics/ Batteries

Electricity is needed on board to supply a wide range of devices, including starters for the engine, pumps, lights, horn, appliances and wall sockets. Power is usually supplied from a number of leisure batteries, similar in appearance to car batteries; these will tolerate deeper discharge and heavier recharging – the situation that occurs in a boat as most demand happens while the engine is off in the evening. The batteries are securely fixed in a compartment, usually near the engine, with separate ones for the engine and cabin supplies. They can either provide

12v or 24v DC (the latter created by two 12 volt batteries), which will power appliances designed (often from a caravanning provenance) to run on these low voltages. The engine will charge the batteries up while running, as in a car, although this can be an expensive option on 24v systems.

Mains power can be provided by the same batteries with the inclusion of an inverter, a solid state device that transforms 12v DC into 230v AC, or a converter where a motor powers an internal mains generator. The quality of the supply produced can vary and only better quality devices may permit most devices from home to be used, and power is not sufficient for high wattage appliances such as electric kettles and heaters. Mains can also be produced by a separate petrol or diesel generator, a noisy but cheap and portable option. Many marinas and private moorings provide a mains socket beside the canal into which a shoreline fitted in the boat can simply be plugged when stationary.

Another option, which is viable if you are very careful with consumption, is wind or solar power. A wind generator mounted on a mast and slotted into sockets on the boat when moored is a common sight these days, although fitting solar panels on the roof can provide a back up on a still day. The initial cost and ravenous consumption by many families mean these are not suitable for most boats.

Layout and Rooms

The length of the cabin, the location of doors and windows, and the demands of the services and their regulations all affect the layout of the interior. However, despite regulations, there is still little standardisation of narrowboat interior plans and there are many variations and personal choices as to where the bulkheads, which divide up the areas, are located. Probably the most common layout, especially on hire boats, is in the following order from the front: the dining/seating area, the galley, the bathroom and a bedroom. On large traditional-style narrowboats with their longer cabin an additional engine or workroom can be squeezed in.

Lounge/Diner

Traditional-style boats look best with portholes along the side and blank panels at the rear, so if any larger windows are fitted it is at the front. This bright and airy space with large glass doors further illuminating the room is where the lounge or diner is sited in this type of boat. This matters less on cruiser-style boats, which tend to have large windows the full length of the cabin and hence the position of the seating area is more flexible, but it is still more commonly found at the front on larger boats. Built-in seats, with their backs fitted under the gunwales, create the maximum space and tables are usually collapsible so that the top can be fitted between seats to make an additional bed.

Kitchen/Galley

Next to this is usually the galley for ease

FIG 6.8: A lounge on a modern narrowboat, featuring a sofa, built-in furniture, a television set and large windows to create a light and warm space.

FIG 6.9: A galley or kitchen with the essential appliances found on most modern narrowboats: cooker, fridge, microwave and sink along with built-in storage cupboards.

of serving food. It can be laid out with a central gangway and two parallel lengths of worktop, or in a U-shape with an offset passage to one side. Compact appliances designed for marine use are generally fitted, although full size white goods can be used where space and power permits. Cookers can be freestanding or built-in and supplied by gas or sometimes diesel. Fridges tend to be special undercounter versions, which can run off electricity or gas, with fridge freezers on some larger craft. Microwaves, dishwashers and even washing machines are fitted on some live-on boats.

Bathroom and Toilets

The bathroom is often an enclosed room with the passage to one side to maximise room, but sometimes on smaller boats the walkway goes through the middle with doors to close it off when in use to save room. A hand-basin, toilet and shower are usually fitted, some larger boats having a compact bath in place of the shower tray. Washing can be a tricky operation on smaller boats and you have to remember to pump out the water after a shower as the tray is below the water level outside.

Constantly a source of amusement and disgust, the toilet on a narrowboat is never as refined as that at home. There are a couple of options for types used, depending upon the method for removing the waste. Most boats use a pump out system, which has a conventional pan, slightly smaller than that at home but usually raised up on a plinth, and when flushed simply opens a flap so that the waste drops into a large tank under the floorboards before

FIG 6.10:
Bathrooms usually have a shower, toilet and hand-basin. Some squeeze in a compact bath.

FIG 6.11:
Bedrooms can feature single beds with a removable centre panel that covers the gap to form a double bed. In others a permanent large bed is fitted with the walkway along one side – as in this example, which shows the same bedroom from each end and includes built-in wardrobes and furniture.

sealing again. When full this is emptied at a pump out station (usually at a marina or boatyard) where a large pipe is fitted into a screw-capped hole along the gunwale and the waste is literally sucked out!

An alternative, which saves space and expense and is used on all sizes of boat, is a cartridge or Elsan toilet. In its basic form it is literally a large bucket with a seat, although in most cases today it has a compact tank called a cartridge below the pan, which is sealed off after use like a pump out toilet. The cartridge can simply be pulled out when full and emptied at a canalside Elsan disposal point (see Chapter 8).

Bedroom

Most boats will have a main bedroom area with a fixed double bed and some wall storage or a wardrobe. Sleeping on a narrowboat can be slightly strange for some, depending which way you face – not too bad if you are pointing end to end, but rocking can be unsettling if you are side to side. You probably won't notice this until you get back home after a holiday and find yourself rocking in your bed for a few days!

CHAPTER 7

Decoration

FIG 7.1: *The intensely colourful nature of traditional narrowboat decoration is the principal part of the appeal of canals. This is an art form in its own right, but its origins are elusive.*

Of all the features of a narrow-boat the one that is the most instantly recognisable is its colourful painting scheme. The stylised roses and the romantic views of lakes, mountains and castles, geometric patterns, barber's shop stripes and bold signwriting create a picture that is unique to these craft. Modern narrowboats can be decorated as the owners wish, with occasionally stylish – or garish – results; however, most still try and incorporate elements of the traditional decoration, and quite often as near to the complete working boat scheme as the new craft will allow. It is to these traditional working boats that you need to look to see where this inspiration came from and the variety that developed.

No one really knows where or when exactly this form of boat decoration

first appeared, but it seems to have developed into the forms we are familiar with by the mid 19th century. Images of earlier craft are rare and often inaccurate; those that can be trusted seem to show elements of the decorative scheme but in a more plain, corporate form. It is in the records of journeys aboard narrowboats that appear in the mid Victorian period that the 'roses' and 'castles' are mentioned in such a way to imply they were commonplace by then.

It is surprising with such a relatively recent art form, developed in well documented times, for there to be no clues about its origin. It is unlikely to have had anything to do with gypsies – the narrowboat had become widespread up to a century before their colourful waggons did. The schemes and form of decoration they used is also completely different upon closer examination. There are elements that can be traced in maritime history; medieval ships were colourfully decorated using heraldic symbols and some later river craft from around Europe used geometric patterns. There may well have been some tradition, which has long been forgotten, for painting river boats in this country and as it was the same builders who worked on the early canals they brought this with them.

One element of the decoration, roses and castles, was probably used by the first families moving on board number ones around the turn of the 19th century, to make the cabin more homely. They may have done it themselves or used a local painter of household goods

FIG 7.2: *There are no constraints to the colour scheme chosen on a modern narrowboat as long as the black and white BWB registration number is displayed upon the cabin side. It is worth noting, however, that the future value of a boat may be affected by the colours and traditional schemes based upon old working boats are more likely to attract sellers than garish or pastel colour decoration.*

FIG 7.3: *The stages of painting roses. The outline is first sketched out in chalk, then the background to the flowers and leaves, before the sweeping brushstrokes of the petals are applied. The final stage is painting on the fine details like stems. The artist would usually paint one stage then move along the boat tackling other decoration before returning to complete the next stage. Working round the boat like this enabled the skilled painter to complete a whole boat in a day or two.*

to copy the popular forms of decoration at the time on pottery, furniture and clocks. These were stylised bunches of flowers and classical scenes of mountains, lakes and romantic follies, clearly using the same simple brush-strokes and compositions as the roses and castles. At some point this relatively quick form of decoration was offered by the boat builders and in a short space of time spread out from its origins in the Midlands to be an accepted practice over the whole network.

Although the decoration seems the same at first glance there are differences between the boatyards and on closer inspection the style of flower and scene painted can be associated with individual artists. Most of these learnt their trade as apprentices and may have

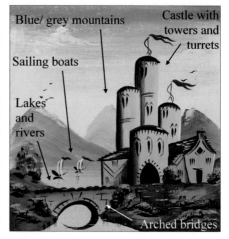

FIG 7.4: *There were a wide variety of styles of castles, depending on the artist and area, with some looking more like churches than fortifications. Some of the most common features that can be found are labelled above.*

FIG 7.5: *Examples of different styles of roses and castles. There are many particular features associated with local areas and boatyards, which can be spotted by the experienced eye. For instance, the style of rose tends to be more realistic around the Potteries and daisies were often incorporated into the bunch in the North, although these features could be found elsewhere.*

combined their work with other boat-building tasks. The best in the trade could complete most of the decoration of a boat in a single day!

On craft owned by companies there would have been a general external colour scheme and style of signwriting used, but other areas would have been decorated in the same way as the number ones. This may have been more limited as it was usual for the owners to pay for the external decoration and just a basic scumble finish in the cabin and for the boatman to pay for any additional painting inside. Day boats, which only travelled a short distance, had smaller cabins and the boatmen often changed from one boat to another, particularly in areas such as Birmingham, so there was little need to personalise a particular craft. These narrowboats had the signwriting on the cabin side and may have used some of the general geometric decoration but rarely anything more elaborate, except on some tugs.

THE DECORATIVE PARTS

Working boats developed a pattern of decoration on their various parts, which, despite different owners' colour schemes and regional variations in style, was remarkably consistent in its general appearance. These elements can still be seen on preserved narrowboats and are copied in part on their modern cruiser counterparts. Whichever colours are chosen, the one golden rule for creating a traditional scheme is to use contrast, with dark shades against light. Most work is in a strong red, green, blue or yellow, with black and white used

FIG 7.6: *A typical font used for the signwriting on the cabin sides. From the late 1790s it was a regulation to put name, home and owner in black and white on the side of the boat. This later developed into full size writing.*

FIG 7.7: *Examples of company liveries on the cabin sides of traditional working narrowboats. Some were occasionally painted on the cratch, like this Ovaltine advert example.*

within colourful patterns and as a background to some decorative parts. So, for instance, a red panel surrounded by a green frame is best edged with a light colour like yellow between them. This originally helped emphasise the geometric shapes used in part to help identify a boat from a distance.

The bow

The first notable splash of colour you see as a traditional narrowboat approaches is on the top bend (the uppermost part of the hull each side of the stem post). Here, seemingly imitating the eyes of the boat used on ancient craft, is an arrangement of diamonds and circles or a number of more unique shapes, usually on a white

FIG 7.9: *An example of a decorated bow (top) and a mast and uprights (below).*

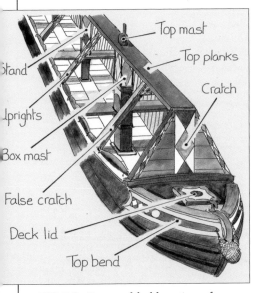

FIG 7.8: *Bow and hold section of a working narrowboat, with labels highlighting the key decorated parts.*

background and nearly always with a crescent shape finishing off the rear end. Above this on working boats, and modern ones where they have been fitted, was the cratch, the triangular upright board that supports the front end of the cover. The most common decoration for this was a vertical band of diamonds down the middle with the right-angled triangular shape either side filled with flowers. The foredeck hatch or deck lid usually contained a simple symbol like a circle or heart set within a square-shaped white base which resembled a piece of stretched canvas on top of the rectangular green lid.

The hold

The main body of a working narrowboat was open with a framework of diagonal uprights, vertical stands and the mast supporting the gang planks, and black tarpaulin sheet over the top of the cargo. The mast was decorated with a diamond pattern on the lower box and telescopic top section; the thinner stands behind and in front of it could repeat the same pattern or be plain with just the upper part decorated. The uprights were usually plain except for the fore pair, which were more visible and would have a diamond pattern, sometimes with a small section of flowers. Where the gangplanks met the rear cabin there was a block, the cabin block, which was also decorated, especially the side facing the boatman steering at the rear. This might be a simple diamond pattern on the motor boat as the block was small, but on buttys with their lower cabin it could be larger and feature roses or castles.

The stern and cabin exterior

The rear of the boat presented the onlooker with an even more elaborate display. The rounded end of the motor's hull, the counter, was usually finished with two or three bands of red, white and on the latter option one of blue, with the front edge of these in a crescent shape. The more elegant tapered end of the butty would have similar treatment to the fore end sometimes, with an additional splash of

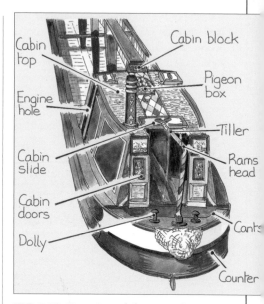

FIG 7.10: *Drawing of the rear of a working motor narrowboat, with labels of the principal decorative parts.*

decoration adjacent to the stern post. The large wooden rudder or elum on buttys was a riot of colour, often with a blue circle draped over its top edge (the ram's head) and a motif like a daisy or a circle on its flanks. The more plain figure-of-seven-shaped tiller on the motor was typically painted with diagonal bands like a barber's shop sign, with the pattern continuing along the upper part, or fitted with a removable brass tube and a varnished wooden handle.

The rear cabin of a working boat had bold sign-written sides, usually divided into two or three panels. On the motor the most common arrangement was to have the boat name in the first, the owner and home port in the second and if there was a third it could be filled with a castle or similar scene. As the butty usually had the boat name on the top bend of the stern it had

FIG 7.11: *A decorated motor cabin (top) and a butty (bottom). The lower view shows a boat in British Waterways livery dating from the 1950s and 60s. In order to save costs they experimented with stick-on printed castle scenes and decoration (used on the open doors in this example) but these imitations were not popular.*

just two panels. The upper line of text was arched upwards on most examples, with the lower usually straight. With the pair of doors shut on the rear of the cabin a distinctive symmetrical pattern was presented, with different companies using their own shapes to identify their craft. These odd but attractive designs probably originated from similar ones that featured on open-topped wagons which were used for haulage in the early 19th century. When the same doors were opened they displayed beautifully decorated panels, the upper raised one with a castle and the central recessed one with roses. When shut these faced inwards, adding to the decorative interior.

The cabin interior

Despite the interior decoration being at the whim of the boatman and his wife there are many similarities between most boats, perhaps in part due to the very limited space for it and the speed with which it had to be painted, so limiting artistic flair. As most wood used inside the cabin was a soft variety it was always painted and combed (scumbling or graining) to give the impression of a better quality finish (this was common on most household woodwork in the 19th century). On top of this a castle scene or similar was painted on the outer face of the drop-down table, with roses on selected drawers and door fronts. On the opposite side, panels filled with roses and another castle if there was a seat end were common. When the outer and engine room doors were closed their decorative faces with castles and roses would complete the intimate and richly colourful interior. The area behind the stove was one of the few hanging spaces and lace plates, brasses and family photos were displayed here.

FIG 7.12: *Decorative details from the interior of working narrowboats. Surrounding the decoration on all the interior surfaces was scumbling (a form of graining), a method of making a wood effect using paint and combs. Typically the surface is painted a cream colour and then a darker brown stain is applied and stroked with a comb while wet to make the desired pattern. It was common in Victorian houses for poorer quality woods to be grained to make them look superior.*

SECTION III

ENJOYING NARROWBOATS TODAY

CHAPTER 8

Hiring and Cruising

FIG 8.1: CALDON CANAL, STAFFORDSHIRE: *One of the first ways that most people are introduced to canal cruising is by hiring a boat for a holiday. Well equipped and attractive, the modern hire narrowboat makes for a relaxing break with most of the creature comforts of home.*

HIRING

Where to hire

There are hundreds of boatyards around the canal network where narrowboats small and large can be hired out for holidays. Most choose a week or two but some hire bases will offer shorter breaks if boats are available. You will get in effect a floating self-catering holiday cottage so

all you will need to do is fill the narrowboat up with diesel, buy your supplies and away you go.

The first decision is which part of the country you would like to cruise in; Fig 8.2 shows the current network but more detailed canal maps are available at boatyards, bookshops or online. The most popular waterway is the Llangollen Canal and hence at peak times it can be overcrowded and slow in places, but the drama is well worth the wait! Other personal favourites of mine include the Leeds & Liverpool, the Caldon Canal in Staffordshire, the Leicester section of the Grand Union Canal, the Oxford Canal and the Kennet & Avon. However, there isn't an ugly canal on the network or one that doesn't in places surprise or delight. These days even the routes through the major cities are welcoming.

If you have set your heart on completing a ring of canals or reaching a set point, then it will be important to get a detailed map of your route so you can check it is achievable in the time you have or ask a hire base who will be able to advise you if it is realistic. As a rough guide you can average around 2–3 mph, take 10–15 minutes through each lock and cruise 7–8 hours a day without pushing yourselves. Some will go quicker or cruise longer but this rather misses the point of a relaxed holiday!

At the same time as choosing your area it is best to start looking at hire bases as their locations may not correspond with your route. The best place to look has always been in magazines, most notably *Waterways World* and *Canals & Rivers*, which along with an increasing number of new publications should be available in newsagents. Most hire bases are now online so the internet is another source. It is also worth checking the British Waterways website (www.britishwaterways.co.uk) or the magazines, especially if travelling early or late in the season when there might be closures of canals for maintenance.

FIG 8.2: *The current canal network runs from Bath in the south-west over to Guildford in the east, up to Yorkshire and across to Lancaster in the west. Navigable canals are indicated by black lines, rivers by blue. This is only a rough guide and you may need to check as to the suitability of your boat for navigating them. There may be a specific canal you wish to cruise on – if not, then it is probably a good idea to choose one of the areas where the canals are numerous, which can provide a convenient ring for your holiday or plenty of options if you just want to wander!*

All boats have to have a British Waterways licence, which should ensure they have been inspected and have

FIG 8.3: *Many hire bases are established in old wharfs and boatyards like this example on the Trent & Mersey Canal at Shardlow.*

reached the required safety standard. Hire bases vary in size from just a couple of boats to a small fleet owned by larger companies. Few actual boatyards, however, are large enough to hold many in one place, so do not expect a massive choice of sizes in one location – you may have to compromise on your holiday area or the size of boat and hence price. Many hire basins are also working boatyards, so don't be put off if they look a bit rough and ready. Check that they provide secure car parking for your vehicle for the duration of the holiday and what they include in the price, for example a full tank of diesel and gas cylinders.

Before casting off

Before setting off you should check that you have the following items. A British Waterways key (the organisation is often known by the initials BW or by its former title BWB), which permits boaters to access sanitary stations and occasionally a lift bridge or lock (to protect it from misuse by non boaters), is essential. There should be two windlasses (also known as lock keys), which will have square holes at the end to raise paddle gear on locks and occasionally a lift or swing bridge. On top of the cabin there should be a long wooden pole with a metal hook at the end, essential for retrieving items and getting the boat out of mud. Also make sure that mooring pins and a hammer are stored somewhere inside. Maps should be provided, or purchased if not; these dedicated canal guides will be necessary to show where water points, sanitary stations, boatyards and moorings are. Finally check there is a crew – it is easy to leave someone behind but not so easy to go back and pick them up if it's your first time at the controls! Make sure that those who cannot swim are wearing a life jacket at all times while outside. Children should be made aware of the dangers that are inherent around a boat and the canals, especially at locks and weirs where they should stay away from the edge and not run about. Everyone should also be careful when getting on and off the boat (try and step on vertically rather than push out) and keep children away from the gap between it and the bank. Canals are generally very safe and enjoyable if these few precautions are heeded.

If someone does fall in then 'don't panic captain'! Act promptly, especially if it is between the boat and the bank when the boat needs to be pushed out as far as the ropes will allow for the unfortunate person to resurface. The canal bottom is not very deep, no more than 3 ft at the sides and rarely more than 5 ft in the middle. This will vary more on wider canals, and rivers have the added risk of flow. The one and only time I fell in was while fishing on the front of the boat with my Dad's rod and my first thought on landing in the water was to protect the rod, so I thrust it as high as I could and shouted at my sister to grab it before me. She just stood and laughed as I hadn't noticed that the water had barely come up to my knees!

CRUISING

The following text and illustrations give a general guide from my experience for controlling the boat and negotiating features along the canal. Remember – do not be afraid to ask other boaters if in doubt. The canal network is an amazingly friendly community, usually only too keen to help and advise beginners. Hire bases will also give instructions for the boat before you take it out.

Casting off

Care needs to be taken with casting off (the procedure of pushing the boat out and setting off). Someone mans the front, where they untie the ropes, pull out any mooring pin, and hold the boat to the bank (usually from the handrail on top of the cabin). With the engine running, the same is repeated at the rear and then the driver has to check the canal for any traffic coming either way (let boats pass if close at hand rather than push out in front). If all is clear then the driver holds the tiller and gear lever while the person at the front

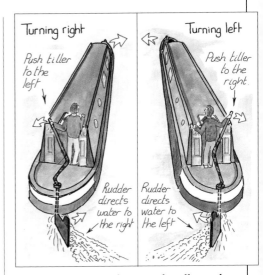

FIG 8.4: *Diagram showing the tiller and rudder and why the boat turns the opposite way to the direction of the tiller.*

gently pushes the boat out a short way, still firmly holding the handrail, and then pulls themselves up onto the gunwale (only a short push is needed to get the boat moving so do not stretch yourself and risk losing your grip). When the front has drifted out clear of any obstructions, the engine can be put in forward gear and given a slow burst of speed until you are in the middle of the canal. The key to any manoeuvring on a narrowboat is the minimum of power and the maximum of time. Do not rush or be rushed, and you should not make a spectacle of yourself!

Steering the boat

Direction is controlled by the tiller, the horizontal arm that is connected below to the rudder. All you need to know about this to get going is that when you move the arm out to the right the front of the boat will turn to the left and vice versa (see Fig 8.4). The gear lever usually controls forward and reverse and the speed all in one, increasing speed the more you push it down in the chosen direction. There is often a small button which, when pressed in, acts as a clutch and disengages the gears so the engine can be run in neutral (usually done when starting in the morning).

Speed

When cruising, remember the following important rules. The maximum speed is 4 mph, a fast walking pace, but you are more likely to be travelling a bit slower. Most boats will not have a speedometer, so speed is generally judged by the wake produced behind you. The faster you go, the higher the waves the boat leaves behind will be. Ideally these should be negligible as they are damaging to the

banks and the repair of these costs millions each year. They will also vary depending upon the depth of water in the canal, so you may find on some that you have to go slower than on wider waterways. As a general rule, go along at a gentle walking pace.

Passing boats

It is also important to slow down when passing moored boats. The displacement of water from your craft passing puts a strain on the ropes holding them in place; any more than a couple of miles an hour and you can rip a poorly tied boat off its moorings and block the canal. Slow down when passing other canal users, especially fishermen – this is partly for good manners as your boat will do little to upset the fish (in fact the churning up of the bottom can encourage them to feed) but excessive wake behind can drain water from the shallow sides where keepnets may be in use and dislodge carefully sited groundbait.

Most important though is to remember that when you meet someone coming in the opposite direction you

FIG 8.5: *The V-shaped wave coming from the boat is known as the wake and will increase in size with speed.*

FIG 8.6: *Always reduce speed when passing moored craft.*

pass them on the **right-hand side**, not the left. It is again polite and easier to control if you slow down when going past.

Bridges, aqueducts and tunnels

When passing under bridges, the canal will often narrow down to a gap only wide enough for one boat to pass. In most cases you can clearly see ahead if anyone is going through but be cautious and approach slowly if you cannot, for example on a sharp bend (if in doubt sound the horn before passing through). When steering through a tight gap like a bridge or lock, it is usually best to line up one side only rather than hop from one to the other. When going under an arched bridge, it is usual to guide yourself along the towpath side as this will keep the cabin top as far away as possible from the lower part of the arch on the opposite side and allows you to keep an eye on anyone jumping on or off the boat. There is no need to do this

FIG 8.8A: *Most aqueducts are only wide enough for one boat to pass along, as in this example at Chirk on the Llangollen Canal. Check that no one is in the channel before entering.*

under larger bridges where there is no narrowing of the canal.

Most aqueducts are single channels so you will have to check for boats coming the other way before proceeding. Many are short and this is little different from a bridge but some – such as the spectacular Chirk and

FIG 8.7: *Line up the towpath side of the gap when passing under narrow bridges to keep the boat as near to the centre as possible.*

FIG 8.8B: *Crossing the Pontcysyllte Aqueduct at the end of the Llangollen Canal is the highlight of most people's holidays and hair-raising for those of us afraid of heights.*

FIG 8.9: *Tunnels were always my favourite part of a trip – going underground into the dark, mysterious space with dripping roof and the occasional shaft of light was great fun when young. For those who are terrified at the thought, most tunnels still have the old towpath for horses running over the top of the hill and occasionally through the actual tunnel for them to use instead. This example is the Harecastle Tunnel on the Trent & Mersey with James Brindley's abandoned tunnel on the far right and Thomas Telford's later replacement on the left. Due to mining subsidence this too has sunk and timed entry is applied for boats travelling through.*

Pontcysyllte Aqueducts (Fig 8.8) need more care. It is worth noting that those without a head for heights may prefer to walk along the towpath. There is no railing on the boat side!

Tunnels can either be a narrow or wide bore, the latter allowing boats to pass within (on the right-hand side). It is usually obvious when approaching the tunnel if it is going to be wide enough for two, although signs will warn you if

not. In this case you will simply have to look for a light in the tunnel and should you see one wait for the boat to emerge before entering. On longer narrow tunnels where this is not possible there will be a timed entry system so boats cannot meet in the middle (see Fig 8.9). Turn your headlight on when entering the tunnel (the switch is usually on the control panel at the back) and keep to the middle to avoid clashing with the sides until meeting another boat coming the other way, when you pull over to the right-hand side to pass. Most tunnels have water dripping down especially around air shafts. Do not be alarmed but wearing a coat and hat might be a good idea.

Getting stuck!

Sometimes due to a build up of silt or low water levels the boat can come to a halt on the soft mud on the bottom of the canal, known as going aground. Do not try and force your way further into it but stop and firstly try to reverse out the way you approached it. The boat would have scoured a channel in the mud and you may simply be able to withdraw backwards. This may be

FIG 8.10: *A very useful tool for when the boat becomes stuck is the pole. There should be one or two on the roof, which can be used carefully to help push the boat out.*

aided by someone pushing the boat back into the channel with the pole on the roof. Be careful when doing this as it can easily become stuck in the mud. Getting the crew to stand all on the side in the deepest water can help, or if you are really stuck then gently rocking the boat may do the trick.

Weed or something man-made like rope getting tied around the prop can affect the boat's performance or at worst stall the engine. If you can see an uneven wake behind the boat or notice a strange judder on the tiller, these are often warning signs. When it is convenient to do so, pull up and turn the engine off, making sure that the gear lever is in neutral.

At the rear of the engine compartment above the propeller will be a weed hatch, a flat steel plate with a screw and some type of bracket holding it in place (see Fig 5.8). Removing this will reveal the water below the counter (this is not part of the hull and it will not cause water to flood in). The only way to remove the obstruction is to roll up your sleeves and reach down into the water. The prop will normally be a foot down and you will have to stretch behind it as most things wrap themselves around the shaft. If the boat stalls when cruising, then again push the gear lever into neutral and ensure the engine is off before removing the hatch. Someone will have to try and control where the boat drifts, either holding it to the far bank with a pole or with ropes if you go onto the towpath side.

Turning around

Most narrowboats will have to turn around at a wider stretch of the canal

FIG 8.11: *Turning the boat around in a specified wide part of the canal is usually best done by (1) pointing the bow into the hole and slowly turning into it so that the boat is at right angles across the canal (this keeps the propeller and rudder in deeper water); (2) then turning the tiller the other way and reversing out until the boat is facing the direction in which it came; (3) then, as the boat is in this photo, putting the engine into forward and returning along the way you came.*

or in a special winding hole (a purpose-built pool in which a boat can turn around or 'wind' in, pronounced as in 'winding' up a clock). These are usually marked on maps and need to be noted when planning a trip as there can be long stretches between them. After ensuring the way is clear, all you need to do is slow down and turn the boat so that the bow (front) goes into the winding hole, keeping the rear in the main canal (this is because the winding holes are usually shallow). When you are far enough in, then put the engine into reverse and turn the tiller the opposite way and the boat should withdraw out, facing the opposite way.

Mooring

Mooring spaces are provided at certain popular places, especially near towns and villages. They are often marked on maps and on the ground will typically have steel piling or concrete banks to show where it is deep enough to pull in. You can moor almost anywhere along the side of canals but you will have to check the depth and the bank is often unsuitable. Never moor up for the night in a short pound between locks or across a weir or where instructed not to. The rules for mooring are different

FIG 8.12: *If you are fortunate, mooring rings (left) may be set in the bank; if not, you will have to hammer in metal pegs front and rear to tie up to.*

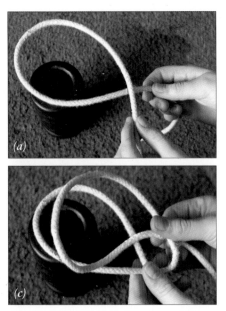

FIG 8.13: *The knot I always used for tying the boat up was as follows. Make a loop (a) and then a second one below it (right in the photo) (b) then move the lower loop above the first (c) and place over the stud or dolly on the boat (d) before pulling the ends tight (e).*

and more limited on rivers, so check when cruising these.

It is usually best to go front first into a space; you can reverse in but many boats have a mind of their own when going backwards! Slow the boat down and turn the bow into the chosen spot. Someone can then jump off with the ropes at the front when near enough and the boat can be put into reverse to bring it to a stop. Then with the person on the bank holding the front (or centre rope where fitted) use gentle bursts of reverse or forward as required to bring the back in. When roughly in place, turn the engine off, put the gear lever into neutral and then step off with the stern rope.

Once the boat is moored up you have to tie it to the bank. Most designated mooring spaces will have metal rings or concrete bollards to which to tie the boat. If not then the boat should be provided with a hammer and a couple of steel mooring pins (around 2 ft long with a flat top and sometimes a loop). These are best

hit into the ground slightly forwards and behind the boat to hold it in place better, although the ground may not permit this. You can share rings and bollards with other boats, but if using their pins make sure you check with them in case they're leaving before you! If the boat has rope fenders along the side (usually left up on the roof when cruising), these need to be dropped down before tying up.

Locks
A lock is the means by which boats climb and descend canals. The basic principle is a bit like an air lock on a submarine. The boat enters a chamber, closing the gates behind it, and then either empties or fills it with water from the next section of canal until both are level, when the gates are opened and it proceeds out. As canals developed as single enterprises a wide range of different style locks and paddle gear developed and although the diagrams illustrate a common form there will be other types to be found in your travels.

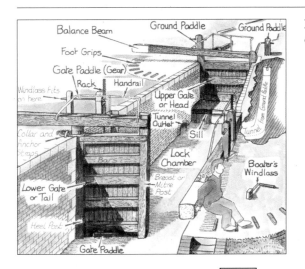

FIG 8.14: *A lock and labels of its parts.*

The main components are the gates, either singles across the full width (usually the top gate, which being shallow does not have too much pressure against it) or a pair mitred at an angle so that the water pressure forces them tight together, preventing leaks and creating a strong seal (mitre gates). Although they weigh several tons the long arms fixed to the top of them counterbalance this so just a small amount of pressure applied to the white painted tip can open them. The other important element is the paddles, which let the water in and out. Locks have either ground paddles, gate paddles or a mix of both. The former are usually positioned to the side of the gates at the top (higher water level) of the lock and raise a sluice gate across a tunnel under-ground, which feeds water from the upper level and into the bottom sides of the lock chamber. Gate paddles are fixed to the gates themselves and raise a wooden sluice covering a hole at the bottom of them (you can usually see the top of it when the chamber is empty).

Paddles are raised and lowered using a windlass or lock key, a right-angled metal bar with two different sized square holes at one end to fit over the corresponding horizontal tapered bar on the paddle gear. It is very important to make sure the windlass is properly on its fitting and not just at the tip. It is also important to make sure the ratchet is resting down into the cog (see Fig 8.15) and not hanging loose as it is this that stops the paddle dropping (you will hear a metal knocking sound when you wind up the paddle if the ratchet is in place). You only lift the ratchet out of the way if

you are lowering the paddle, when you should hold the windlass handle securely. With the best will in the world it will one day slip from your grasp and if you were lowering it at the time will spin round rapidly out of control. DO NOT try and stop or catch it, but stand well back and warn those around you as when it hits the bottom the windlass will invariably fly off. I can speak from experience that it hurts if you try and catch it!

FIG 8.15: *Conventional gate paddles being operated (top). Always make sure the ratchet is on the cog wheel (bottom) to ensure the paddle cannot slip. When lowering you push the windlass up slightly so you can lift the ratchet out of the way and then wind the paddle down carefully.*

FIG 8.16: *Some paddle gear has been replaced in the last century by hydraulic gear. This is safer as the paddle will stay up after it has been raised without the need for a ratchet. The disadvantage is that the hydraulic gear has to be turned with equal effort to lower them!*

Operating locks

Working locks can be fun, but there are hazards. These can generally be avoided if you remember a few simple things. Do not run around the lock, especially when wet, and secondly make sure someone with a windlass next to the open paddles is watching the lock AT ALL TIMES during filling and emptying. This is essential so that the paddles can be promptly dropped if there is a problem or should someone fall in.

When approaching a lock from above or below you must first ensure the level of the water in the lock is the same as that which you are on. If it is not, then you need to check that no one is in view approaching from the other end (if so wait and let them go first, it will save a colossal amount of water). If all is clear, make sure all gates are shut and then raise the paddles at the end nearest your boat to fill or empty the

lock accordingly (the boat should wait a short distance back from the gates, where you will usually find bollards to secure it). The gates are then opened, the paddles lowered and the boat carefully driven in. Make sure that any fenders down the side of the boat are up and out of the way as they can cause a boat to get jammed.

Bring the boat to a standstill in the lock. If going down, keep the bow rope fender up close to the gate ahead; if going up, keep the stern close to the bottom end, just enough for the gates to close behind. This is not essential but helps to avoid the boat getting thrashed around as water is let in and out and it also keeps full-length boats away from the sill that is under the top gate (the boat can either be controlled in the lock

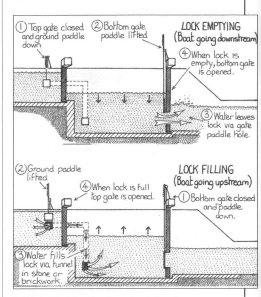

FIG 8.17: *The basic principle of operating a lock.*

by the engine or by a rope thrown around a bollard and held by the driver).

When the gates are shut the paddles at the opposite end can be raised carefully to around halfway. Do not go any further at first as the sudden rush of water will pull on the boat and can force it into the gate. Wait for it to settle and rise a short way before opening them all the way. It is important when filling a lock to open any ground paddles before gate ones; it is best not to open the latter until the water level is over the sill as it can splash into the boat if you are not careful! If you are going up a wide lock on your own, then it is best to raise the ground paddle on the same side as the boat (this will usually hold it to the lock wall rather than pull it off). When the water in the lock is level with that on the other side the gates can be pushed open, the paddles dropped and the boat can leave. Always close the gates if no one else is coming in to prevent water loss (lock gates will swing open a bit when water is level; this is unavoidable and they will slam shut when the paddles are opened).

Swing bridges

These are low level bridges used for footpaths, farm tracks and occasionally roads to cross the canal. There are many different types for numerous situations but they are usually counterbalanced like a lock gate so that pressure applied to the end hanging over the land will swing the part over the canal out the way of the boat.

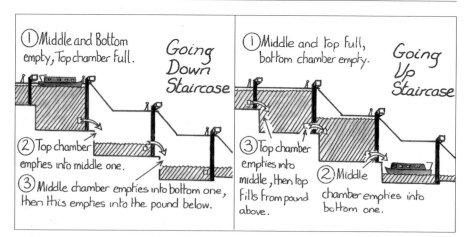

FIG 8.18: *Where space was limited and cost savings were required, locks were grouped together to form a staircase, with the top gate of one acting as the bottom of the next one up. They are usually found in a set of two or three and on narrow canals can only be entered if there are no other boats within them. The Bingley Five on the Leeds & Liverpool Canal and the Foxton flight on the Leicester section of the Grand Union Canal are two notable larger examples.*

FIG 8.19: *Examples of swing bridges open and shut. The top one is operated by a switch panel with safety gates as it is on a busy road. The lower example on a less important route is simply pushed open on the opposite side from the towpath.*

Someone will have to be let off the boat when approaching one and go across the bridge to operate it. Always check that there is no traffic coming and make sure that any chain that keeps the bridge shut is released before starting. You will either have to wind a paddle gear, as on a lock, operate a button (you may need your BW key), or simply push the far end in order for the bridge to swing open. Reverse the procedure to close it afterwards and re-fix any chain to lock it when closed.

Lift bridges

Another type of bridge used in a similar situation is a lift bridge. These may also have a road over them so you may have

FIG 8.20: *A large (top) and smaller (bottom) lift bridge. The top example is electrically operated with traffic lights; the lower example on a farm track is simply raised by pulling a chain on the far side from the towpath.*

to be aware of traffic approaching although most on busier routes will have some form of warning signals triggered when the bridge lifts up. The structures are again counter-balanced either by arms fixed to the bridge similar to those on lock gates or more usually by a high frame with an arm which lifts the deck when a chain is pulled at the other end. The procedure is similar to that for a swing bridge with either paddle gear, electric switches or a chain to be pulled to raise the deck so the boat can pass underneath.

Filling up

At some point on your holiday you will probably have to fill up the boat with water and fuel. Gas cylinders, which are stored in locked metal containers, might also need changing if they run out. This is done by releasing the cap and swapping it with the spare, which should be full. If not, new ones can be bought from boatyards and marinas (you always return the empty one when buying a full cylinder).

Although diesel tanks are often large enough to give weeks of cruising, at some point they need filling (if there is no gauge, a wooden dipstick down through the filler cap can give a reading). The engine's tank is usually at the rear in the engine compartment and is filled through a screw cap on the gunwale above (these can usually be undone by inserting a coin in the slot but be careful to hold the cap as it may not be chained to the boat and could drop into the canal).

Diesel can be purchased from boatyards and marinas and is dispensed via a pump, in the same way as cars. In the past this has been rather cheap as pink agricultural subsidised diesel has been permitted for use in narrowboats. At the time of writing this is being reviewed and change may occur in late 2008, which could see a rise in costs. It may be that pink diesel can still be used for central heating (some boats now have a separate tank for this) but many boatyards have only one pump and will only supply the more expensive type for the engine.

The water tank is filled by a hose (usually stored on the boat somewhere in the front) from canalside water points, which are marked on your map. There will be a screw cap along the gunwale (normally towards the front), which when undone allows the hose to be inserted down the filler pipe a short way and the tap turned on. When the tank is full, water will begin to spurt out of an overflow hole on the side of the hull nearby. Turn the tap off and refit the screw cap.

Emptying toilets

The most common arrangement is for narrowboats to have to pump out with the waste stored in a tank under the toilet. The removal is done at marinas and boatyards who will charge for the service. A large hose is simply fitted into the screw-capped hole on the gunwale next to the bathroom and the waste is pumped out (an air hole in the tank stops it imploding).

Portable toilets are either just a tall bucket or a more elaborate flushable type (by far the most common) with a

FIG 8.21: *At points along the canals, sanitary stations will be found where cartridge-type toilets can be emptied out. These are usually located next to water filling points and are commonly found at junctions, at the top or bottom of flights of locks or at old boatyards. Your BW key will be required to open the door.*

lower cartridge that can be pulled out and carried when it needs to be emptied (this will be more often than a pump out). This task can be unpleasant and a method of choosing the unfortunate person by rota or straws may need to be applied! Canalside sanitary stations are provided at regular intervals, usually along with a water point, at the top of locks or at a boatyard and are free of charge. For some strange reason they are locked – it's hard to imagine who would want to go inside one by choice. The cartridge or bucket is simply poured down the pan inside, then washed out with the tap or hose provided.

> ## FURTHER INFORMATION
>
> The following magazines are a good starting point for finding contacts for hiring (and buying) boats:
>
> *Waterways World*
> *Canals and Rivers*
> *Canal Boat*
> *Narrowboat*
> *Towpath Talk* (can be accessed online)
>
> Further information can also be gained from the internet sites listed at the end of Chapter 9.

Buying and Living on a Narrowboat

FIG 9.1: *There can be few better incentives to either buy or live upon a boat than to wake up in the morning, throw open the front doors and be welcomed by a view like this. What, though, are the things to look out for and the costs of purchasing a narrowboat for holidays or as a home?*

Buying your first boat is a momentous occasion and our family, like other new owners, could not wait to go on its maiden voyage. For most of us in the 1970s the first purchase was a fibreglass craft; in our case four of us packed onto a tiny 16-ft Microplus that barely offered half its length in cabin so my sister and I had to sleep outside under the cover of a leaky tarpaulin. However limited the accommodation, it was with great excitement that we climbed on board for our first trip on the Llangollen Canal, watching Dad firmly sit his captain's hat on his head, fire the engine up and cast off. No sooner had we gone a few hundred yards than he looked down at his feet and noticed a trickle of water lapping along the floor. As is characteristic of all captains in this situation he calmly stated, 'Oh that's strange, a bit of water is getting in,' and then looked up to find himself alone! Our excitement had evaporated with the first mention of 'water' and the crew had already abandoned ship and were standing firm footed on the towpath!

Even though we had cruised hire boats for over ten years and knew the basics of what to look for in a boat there was still an element of risk with this first boat. Dad patched it up and we eventually began our holiday but this and subsequent boats always surprised in some way or other, however well planned the purchase. This chapter gives some basic guidelines to buying narrowboats and planning to live upon one and where to seek more expert advice, but in the end a certain amount of trial and error will be required!

BUYING A NARROWBOAT

Size

The first thing to consider when planning to buy a narrowboat is where you are likely to use it and the room that will be required. These will both affect the length you should start looking at. Some canals have shorter locks than the standard 72 ft and other limitations that may restrict the size and type of boat you are likely to need. Also the number of people that are likely to use the boat and their personal requirements will need to be considered when choosing the length of craft. A

rainy day spent cooped up inside a narrowboat may mean, even if there are only two of you, that extra space will be appreciated!

A shorter length of boat, around 35 ft to 55 ft, will be able to negotiate most parts of the system and generally provide enough space for family holidays. A longer craft of up to 70 ft will be more flexible inside, especially if you are considering living aboard, but will be trickier to manoeuvre and cost more to run as mooring fees and licence charges increase with size. If you have not cruised before it is well worth hiring a boat for a holiday to get a better idea of what will suit you and the length of boat that will suffice.

Where to buy

The next aspect is to consider how much you want to spend and what you can expect for your money. Smaller boats will be cheaper but not necessarily much less than longer narrowboats as they both need the expensive elements fitted like an engine and appliances, it's just that a longer craft has more space. New boats have the advantage of not requiring any immediate maintenance and a hull with the full thickness of steel, less of a risk than a second-hand craft. There will also be options on the fitting out – limited perhaps to choice of décor in the mass-produced market, far more bespoke on the luxury end.

The price of new boats is in constant fluctuation, depending on factors like the price of steel and the state of the market, so if they are out of your range a second-hand boat will be the next

Some points to look out for when buying a boat:

1 AGE: *Unless well looked after, boats over 10 years old will soon need repairs and repainting.*

2 MAKES: *Find out the make of boat – some have good reputations, other less so. Some older makes like Springers were terrific value for money but they were cheap because they were simple and of lower specification.*

3 MATERIALS: *Try and stick to all-steel boats when starting out, steer clear of fibreglass and wood cabins and walk away if the materials used are unknown!*

4 CONDITION: *Do not touch a boat that does not have a current BW Safety Certificate. Be wary of the 'It only needs a few jobs done in places to conform' – why didn't the seller get them done if they were that simple?*

5 SURVEY: *Always have a survey carried out on the boat. This can be arranged by the marina or broker, or by you. Ensure that this includes a comprehensive check of the hull and engine, especially plate thicknesses. Always try and meet the surveyor on the boat to talk through any problems – your surveyor is the only one on your side!*

6 BARGAINS: *If you follow these guidelines you will reduce the chances of buying a boat that requires more work than initially apparent. There are rarely any bargains around – if it's cheap it's for a good reason, especially if sold through a brokerage or marina. If you are still tempted by a tatty old bargain, then budget for extra work and do not expect to get your money back.*

option. In general it is best to stick to a boat under ten years of age as these will have been built under the new safety directives and are less likely to require major maintenance. However, cheaper craft can deteriorate if not looked after, so a survey will be essential whatever the age. Older boats can represent a bargain to first-time buyers but you must allow some money for maintenance, especially to the hull, which at worst could need re-plating. Also, be wary of boats with fibreglass or wooden cabins and hulls – there is nothing intrinsically wrong with them, it is just that these are either prone to leaks or require more regular and specialised work upon them than all-steel craft.

New boats are usually advertised in magazines like *Waterways World* (see the list at the end of Chapter 8), on the internet and sometimes via brokers or marinas. Most boatyards are small and some of the best get a regular turnover from just word of mouth alone so don't be afraid to ask who made a boat that catches your eye. Most second-hand narrowboats are bought at marinas, through brokerage sites, either via magazines or the internet, or privately in the same media. As with buying a car, it pays to look around to see what you get for your money at the approximate length you have chosen.

Other expenses
Before buying, it is worth looking into the cost of running a boat and where it can be moored. Like a holiday home or static caravan, there are fees for keeping your craft at a particular location.

> A summary of current annual costs and expenses for a leisure boat, varying depending on the length and quality required (assumes a couple of weeks' holiday and several weekend journeys):
>
> 1 *Moorings:* £1,000–£2,000
> 2 *BW licence:* £400–£800
> 3 *Insurance:* £200–£400
> 4 *Maintenance:* £500 (includes repainting, batteries, fenders, appliances, and ropes)
> 5 *Diesel:* £200–£400
> 6 *Gas cylinders:* £50
> 7 *Pump out:* £50
> 8 *Electricity from shoreline will be charged similarly to that at home.*

Marinas, boat clubs and other mooring sites will usually charge per foot of length and you should expect to pay the full annual fee to keep your spot even if you are away cruising for much of the time. Marinas tend to be the more expensive option but generally offer better facilities and security. Boat clubs are probably the cheapest and are a great way to meet others with a similar passion but do not be surprised if there is a waiting list, and clubs are usually keen to welcome those who want to contribute to the social side as well as gain a mooring. If you choose an alternative private site – usually along the opposite side from the towpath – it will probably save money. However, check that the access to your mooring is sound and large enough so that you can get your car close by for unloading, and find out if it has power points close at hand to operate power tools and appliances when you are not cruising. Also be aware that in some areas people might choose to target your boat; boards across towpath-side windows can keep stones out and extra security on all openings might be worth considering.

All boats on the canal system need a BW licence, which is charged like moorings by the length of the craft. Insurance is a requirement and there are brokers and companies who specialise in marine cover. The internet and magazines are a good place to search for this. Also remember to allow for the cost of diesel, gas cylinders and pump out while you are cruising. Even a new boat will need repainting at regular intervals; it is usual for a boat to be put into a dry dock every three years or so for cleaning and blacking.

Fitting out your own boat

It is worth remembering that, as with a caravan or car, the value of your boat is likely to drop over time. This will not be an investment but if chosen carefully and regularly maintained will not wear out as quickly as these other options will. An alternative is to fit out a boat yourself. Building from scratch is best forgotten, but fitting out the interior can save money and allow you to customise decoration. I would not, however, recommend this unless you have experience with boats and are competent in most aspects of carpentry, gas, fitting, electrics and plumbing. There are many half-completed projects up for sale as a result of those of us who thought we knew it all finding we didn't!

If you have set your heart on this route, then most people who fit out a boat will buy the hull and super-structure, usually with an engine fitted and some of the heavy work, like the installation of windows, completed (advertised by boat builders as 'sailaway' prices). You will also have to find and pay for moorings or hard standing with access for vehicles and a mains power socket close at hand for power tools. Cost in for professional advice and surveys, and the gas must be installed by a Corgi registered fitter. Do not try any unusual layouts but follow professionally fitted out boat plans.

LIVING ON A NARROWBOAT

There can be few more attractive places to live than on a narrowboat. Waking up in the morning, swinging open your front doors and watching the sun rising over tree-lined canals and wisps of mist floating over tranquil waters, accompanied by the sound of bird song. The boat is open to the elements in summer and warm and cosy in winter. You can stay put at your home mooring or spend a life cruising when the weather suits and tying up in different places when it doesn't.

In the past, living on a narrowboat was always seen as a cheap option, especially in major cities where some sites and poorly maintained craft gave it a bad name in the eyes of authorities. This is no longer the case as a wide range of age groups choose to live on custom-fitted boats with the same luxuries, facilities and standards as a land-based home. This, however, comes at a price and living on a boat while conforming to regulations and authorities means it is not as cheap as it once was.

The boat

Many sell up their home and use the money from this to buy a good boat, with the balance being invested for the future. Others might keep their land property, perhaps renting it out – a good idea if feasible as the boat will lose value, making it very hard to get back onto the housing market if a life afloat does not suit you.

Make sure that the boat is large enough. There is no way you can visualise the reduction in space in a narrowboat. If you've never owned a boat then it is vital to first hire one of a similar size to that which you feel will suit you. Instead of thinking of it as a holiday, try and imagine using the space as your home. Storage is the biggest problem, particularly if you are still working. It is a tough decision to decide on length – do you go for a 55-ft craft, which will allow you to cruise everywhere, or a 70-ft one, which gives the extra space but limits your route?

You will need power, inverters or converters and a shoreline to connect up to the mains when you're on home moorings. You will probably want to consider central heating, and perhaps a solid fuel stove in addition. You might find that the usual built-in seating under the gunwale gives an ache in the neck for regular use. Freestanding chairs in an open lounge area are worth considering despite the loss of space.

Moorings

Perhaps the most important consideration is where to moor. The authorities prefer you to have a registered home base and in addition to some marinas and boatyards that offer live-aboard mooring there are a number of BW purpose-built sites for this. Demand is high, though, and you may have to wait a year or two to get what you want, so check it out before committing to a boat.

Make sure the site has power to the mooring berth and access and parking for a car. You will want to think about how far you have to go to get water, diesel and empty your toilet. A marina may offer this on site, but if not you might have to travel quite a way in the depths of winter when the canal at worst could be iced solid! Boats can have washing machines and tumble dryers on board but this is not always convenient so a local launderette could be important. Although rural locations may seem idyllic, being close to a town or even located in a major city can have big advantages and still have surprisingly tranquil surroundings.

> **Current average annual costs for living aboard after you have purchased the boat which will probably be in the region of £35,000–£100,000 are:**
>
> 1 *The mooring: £2,000–£4,000*
> 2 *BW licence: £800–£1,400*
> 3 *Diesel, pump out and gas (heating is the biggest cost): £1,000*
> 4 *Electricity tie up charges: Same as at home*
> 5 *Residential boat insurance: £300–£500*
> 6 *Maintenance charge: £500*
> 7 *Mobile telephone charges: Remember to include your usual home use and internet as they will have to go through your mobile.*
> 8 *Council Tax: Usually charged as Band A for a boat.*

CONTACTS

The Residential Boat Owners Association (RBOA) is the best source of information on living aboard a boat. Their book *Living Afloat* is available from: PO Box 267, Ely, CB7 9EP (website: www.rboa.org.uk).

The following internet sites contain general information on buying and living on narrowboats:
www.canaljunction.com
www.waterways.org.uk (IWA site)
www.canalcuttings.co.uk
www.canalboat.co.uk
www.canals.com
www.ukcanals.net/mag.html

You could also try the magazines listed at the end of Chapter 8.

GLOSSARY

ANODES: Lozenge-shaped pieces of a metal that is more prone to corrosion than steel, hence they are corroded in the slightly acidic canal water before the hull (also known as 'sacrificial' anodes).

BOATYARD: A canalside works where boats are built or fitted out. Often offers a dry dock where boats can have their hulls cleaned and repainted. May also offer diesel and pump out.

BOLLARD: A short metal, wooden, or concrete post beside a lock or moorings for tying up the boat.

BOW: The front of a boat. On the inland waterways this term is rarely used, it is simply referred to as 'the front'.

BOW THRUSTER: A transverse mounted motor in the front of a narrowboat, which gives the driver extra control of the bow of a boat.

BW: British Waterways (formerly known as BWB – British Waterways Board) are the body largely financed by taxes to maintain the canal network.

CAULKING: The traditional method of forcing a thin piece of rope or hessian soaked in linseed oil (known as 'oakum') into the narrow seams between planks on a wooden hull to make them watertight.

COUNTER: An extension of the rear of the boat across the propeller, which keeps it surrounded by water so it does not lose thrust. The counter is the part of a motor-powered narrowboat rear that you see above water and stand upon.

CRATCH: A triangular-shaped vertical board fitted to the front of working boats which supported the top planks and covered the front end of the hold. It is often fitted as a decorative feature on modern narrowboats to support the cover over the front hold.

CUT, THE: Another term for the canal.

DOLLY: A short cylindrical post welded onto the back of the boat for securing ropes.

ELUM: The large decorated rudder on a traditional unpowered narrowboat.

GREASER: A metal tube, vertically mounted close to the prop shaft at the rear of the engine, which when turned forces grease into the shaft to keep it watertight. Usually needs to be turned a short way on a regular basis.

GUNWALE: The narrow ledge along the side of a boat, which you can walk along whilst holding the handrail on the top of the cabin (also GUNNEL).

HATCH: Either hinged or sliding horizontal openings.

KEEL: A vertical board fitted lengthways up the hull of a sailing boat to prevent it turning over. They were fitted to river craft but not permanently fitted to narrowboats.

KEELSON: The central wooden beam down the floor of a working boat to which the planks and mast were fixed. It derives its name from the similar beam in sailing boats to which the keel was fitted.

LIFT BRIDGE: A bridge that is hinged one side and lifts out of the way when a boat passes beneath (e.g. Tower Bridge).

LOCKS: The means by which boats go up and down hills. The type used today are pound locks, which have a chamber with watertight gates at both ends and paddles that can be raised to let water in and out.

MARINA: A canalside business, which has a chandler's (a shop selling boat parts and fittings), services like pump out and diesel and usually offers secure long-term moorings.

MOORING: The act of tying the boat up alongside the canal bank, or in plural form the place where you can do so.

MOORING PINS: Large metal nails or pins with a flattened head and sometimes a loop near the top, which are hammered into the canal bank to tie the ropes to when mooring.

NUMBER ONES: A term applied to traditional working boats which were owned and run by boatmen rather than a carrying company.

OAKUM: The thin sliver of rope or hessian soaked in linseed oil which was forced into gaps on a wooden hull (see CAULKING).

PADDLES: A vertical board, usually hidden from view, which covers openings in lock gates and in the ground at the top and is raised to let water through. They are lifted by turning the paddle gear above ground using a windlass or lock key.

PIGEON BOX: A small box shaped like a squat house, sometimes with portholes in the roof section, which sits on the cabin roof, originally to ventilate the engine room, but now often used mainly for decoration.

PILING: Vertical sheets, today usually steel, driven into the edge of the canal to protect the canal bank from the wake produced by boats and damage from animals. The space behind is backfilled with mud often dredged up from the canal.

PINTLE: A metal pin bracketed off a surface by a bar onto which a door or shutter could be hinged. In the case of a horse-drawn narrowboat, it was used to hang the rudder from.

PUMP OUT: A form of toilet with a tank below the floor, which is pumped out by, in effect, a large vacuum cleaner via a hose fixed into a hole on the gunwale. This service is provided at boatyards and marinas.

RAM'S HEAD: The upper part of the rudder on a horse-drawn narrowboat (see Fig 2.4).

SANITARY STATION: A small canalside building in which cartridge or Elsan-type toilets can be emptied out.

SCARF JOINTS: A joint to fix two planks end on by making a diagonal cut on each which interlocked. This makes a much stronger joint than just butting them up and was used on wooden narrowboat hulls.

SKEG: The horizontal beam below the propeller, which holds the bottom of the rudder in place.

STEM POST: The curving vertical post at the very front of the narrowboat.

STUD: A T-shaped metal fitting on the front deck and sometimes on the cabin top or at the rear, to which ropes are tied.

SWIM: The section of the hull that curves in to form the front and rear of a narrowboat and whose shape and profile determines how smoothly the boat passes through water and how well it manoeuvres.

SWING BRIDGE: A low horizontal bridge that swings out of the way of boats when the half that is over the land is pushed.

TILLER: The upper part of a rudder, which you hold to steer the boat. These are usually removable so they do not cause an obstruction when not in use and are held in place by a tiller pin.

TUMBLEHOME: The inward sloping profile of the top section of the hull and the cabin sides.

WEED HATCH: A hole in the counter covered by a metal plate held in place by bolts, which permits access to the propeller – when the engine is switched off and out of gear – to clear any rubbish it may have picked up.

WINDING HOLE: A purpose-built widened section of the canal or pool in which a boat can turn around or 'wind' in (pronounced as in 'winding' up a clock).

WINDLASS: Also known as a lock key. A right-angled metal bar with one or two square holes at one end that fit onto the paddle gear on locks to enable the paddles to be raised or lowered. Can also be used to operate some bridges.

INDEX